MW01126700

MOTHER
of EXILES

"Suspension Bridge"
James W. Pace III

JAMES PACE

MOTHER of EXILES

INTERVIEWS OF ASYLUM SEEKERS
AT THE GOOD NEIGHBOR SETTLEMENT HOUSE, BROWNSVILLE, TEXAS

Angelus

To the thousands of courageous asylum seekers.

–JWP

William J. Clinton Presidential Library, *Remarks by the President in Roundtable Discussions on Peace Efforts, National Palace of Culture, Guatemala City, Guatemala* [Press Release]. The White House, Office of the Press Secretary. (1999, March 10). In the public domain. Used with Permission.

CONTRIBUTORS
Sarah Towle, *Introduction*
Dan Bonner, *Benediction*
Sandra Milagros (a pseudonym), *Trauma Never Forgotten*, edited by James Pace
Andrea Rudnik, *Message Not Received*, and coauthor
with James Pace of *Hard-fought Struggle*
Marianela Ramírez Watson, *excerpts from interview* by James Pace
Jack M. White Jr. MSW, *The Good Neighbor Settlement House's Refugee Respite Program,*
edited by James Pace

INTERVIEW METHODOLOGY
All of the interviewees were informed of the purpose and use of each oral history, voluntarily agreed to participate in the interview, and consented to its immediate public dissemination. Many of the interviewees used pseudonyms for the purpose of publication. The author obtained oral consent for each interview. The interviewees did not receive remuneration. No part of this book may be used for reprint, photocopying, scanning, digital media, social media, or distribution of it in any form without written permission.

LIBRARY OF CONGRESS CATALOGING-IN-PUBLICATION DATA
Name: James Pace, author.
Title: Mother of exiles: interviews of asylum seekers
at the good neighbor settlement house, brownsville, texas/James Pace.
Description: Angelus Artists Productions, Inc. City of Publisher : St. Louis, 2022
ISBN 978-1-7379208-0-9 (hardcover) | ISBN 978-1-7379208-2-3 (paperback)
ISBN 978-1-7379208-1-6 (ebook)
Subjects: Nonfiction
Religion/Christianity/Social Issues/Political Science/Geopolitics/Asylum
Seekers/ Brownsville, Texas/Matamoros, Mexico/US Settlement Houses

First Edition, 2022
Copyright © 2022 James Pace
Edited by Suzanne Pace
Cover and Interior Design by 1106 Design
Printed in the United States of America

Angelus
Artists Productions, Inc.
Publisher
8016 Clayton Lane Ct
St. Louis, Missouri 63105
AngelusArtistsProductions@gmail.com

CONTENTS

CHAPTER THREE
GANGS

CONTENTS

CHAPTER FOUR
FAMILY

CONTENTS

Manuel Vilaret/Moment via Getty Images BARBED LIBERTY

INTRODUCTION

Setting the Stage

Once upon a time, not too long ago, the Rio Grande Valley border was porous. Families crossed it regularly, and easily, living binational, bicultural lives. This was the era of "natural migration," with people coming and going between work and home, and crossing from one country to the other to attend a wedding or to receive specialized medical care. Border Patrol agents ushered familiar folks through the international boundary without checking passports. They opened ports of entry when hands were needed in US fields; then waved the workers southward again, now laden with goods purchased in US stores, when the seasonal harvest was over.

In the 1970s and '80s a new population began to arrive at the US frontier, not as part of their daily lives, but to start new ones. This was the era of the "Dirty Wars," when civilians throughout Central America were too often caught in the crosshairs of the violence sweeping their native lands. A thirty-six-year genocidal war in Guatemala decimated the country's indigenous population, leaving two hundred thousand dead or forcibly disappeared. El Salvador's twelve-year conflict, typified by the murder of Catholic Archbishop Óscar

Romero, sent seventy-five thousand souls to the grave, disappeared eight thousand others, and displaced five hundred fifty thousand more. The counterinsurgency, aka Contra War, in Nicaragua, dedicated to checking the advances of the popular revolution there, killed another thirty thousand on top of the fifty thousand sacrificed in the effort to overthrow the brutally repressive, US-supported Somoza-family dictatorship.

Indeed, US fingerprints could be found in each and every twentieth-century Central American contest.[1] Harnessing Cold War rhetoric to whip up historic fears of a Soviet threat right on our doorstep, successive US governments spared no expense to protect US and other foreign investments in the region, even at the cost of lives. Only Honduras escaped armed conflict at that time. But it was no less involved: Its Soto Cano (or Palmerola) Air Base became the staging ground for US-sponsored civil strife in Nicaragua as well as El Salvador.[2] In the process, it addicted corrupt elites and officials to arms and drug trafficking—habits that have undermined regional stability ever since.

LIVING THE GOSPEL, ACCORDING TO MATTHEW

Nearly one million Central Americans arrived at the US border between 1981–1990.[3] But they found the doors of the so-called promised land closed to them. Most were deported right back where they came from, many to certain death.[4]

---

1 Chomsky, Aviva. *Central America's Forgotten History: Revolution, Violence, and the Roots of Migration*, Copyright © 2021 by Aviva Chomsky. (Boston, Massachusetts: Beacon Press, 2021).

2 Ibid., Ch. 7, "Honduras: Staging Ground for War and Reaganomics."

3 Gzesh, Susan. "Central Americans and Asylum Policy in the Reagan Era." Migration Policy Institute, 1 Apr. 2006, https://www.migrationpolicy.org/article/central-americansand-asylum-policy-reagan-era.

4 Sieff, Kevin. "When Death Awaits Deported Asylum Seekers." *washingtonpost.com*, 26 Dec. 2018, www.washingtonpost.com/graphics/2018/world/when-death-awaits-deported-asylum-seekers.

INTRODUCTION

The borderlands faithful found it impossible to reconcile the actions of a government that refused protection to the very victims it created. A movement sprang out of the dry Arizona desert and quickly spread east-west along the two-thousand-mile US-Mexico frontier. Based on the Judeo-Christian principles of welcoming the stranger, healing the sick, and giving water and nourishment to the thirsty and hungry, participating congregations provided sanctuary to the traumatized and destitute pouring into the borderlands. They did so in open defiance of an immigration agenda they felt betrayed both religious beliefs as well as national values, the promise of the US Constitution, and internationally recognized human rights conventions to which the US was a signatory.

At the height of the sanctuary movement, over five hundred houses of worship of all denominations comprised a newfangled overground railroad, willing to support Central American refugees in an act of civil disobedience.[5] In Brownsville, Texas, the Casa Romero, established in 1980 in honor of the slain priest, cared for about one hundred fifty souls each month. Within two years, according to Victor Maldonado, Executive Director of Casa Romero's successor, The Bishop Enrique San Pedro, Ozanam Center, Inc., five hundred to six hundred sought shelter there each day.[6]

The Nineties brought a glimmer of hope to the region, following the fall of the Soviet Union. Peace processes vowed to pursue justice for the worst human rights offenders. President Clinton issued a public apology, stating "that support for military forces or intelligence units which engaged in violent and widespread repression of the kind described in the report [report of the Historical Clarification Commission] was

5 Murphy, Caryle, "Casa Romero: A Safe Port on the Texas Border." *washingtonpost.com*, 4 Sept. 1984, www.washingtonpost.com/archive/politics/1984/09/04/casa-romero-a-safe-port-on-the-texas-border/91053d90-aa03-4f5f-8ccc-ff1f4340c3c4.
6 Maldonado, Victor, Executive Director, The Bishop Enrique San Pedro, Ozanam Center, Inc. *Interview with Sarah Towle*, 13 Aug, 2021, ozanambrownsvillecenter.org.

wrong, and the United States must not repeat that mistake."[7] Trade deals, touted as the answer to economic development and future stability, were sealed. But this was a false promise.

US intervention shifted to imposing economic polices that tilted in favor of the wealthy and against workers and environment. This set off a hemispheric "race to the bottom" in wages, while simultaneously giving right of way to destructive extractive industries. US agricultural surpluses flooding into the region crashed local economies just as international financial investments in mining and hydroelectric power displaced the rural poor. Both phenomena drove millions of small-scale farmers and agricultural workers off the land and into *maquiladoras*. Owned by transnational corporations that were promised low taxes and no regulations, these operations eschewed fair working conditions in favor of positive revenue. The violence of war gave way to the violence of poverty as traditional labor practices went into extinction.

Today, the distribution of wealth in Latin America is among the most unequal in the world, allowing narco-trafficking and its chief bedfellows, corruption and brutality, to spread throughout the Americas without regard for national boundaries. Add climate change to this already toxic mix—with extreme weather events either burning up or drenching the coffee and fruit-growing baskets of the Americas—and you have the perfect storm of root causes of forced migration.

While the reasons for displacement have changed over the years, refugees from Central America, and beyond, have just kept coming. The one thing that remains constant, according to Brownsville native son, James Pace, is that they are running for their lives.

---

7 The White House, Office of the Press Secretary. (1999, March 10). *Remarks by the President in Roundtable Discussions on Peace Efforts, National Palace of Culture, Guatemala City, Guatemala* [Press Release]. Retrieved from https://clintonwhitehouse6.archives .gov/1999/03/1999–03-10-remarks-by-the-president-in-roundtable-in-guatemala.html, William J. Clinton Presidential Library. In the public domain.

Some are 'traditional' asylum seekers, fleeing political persecution, or economic migrants fleeing hardship. But in this last decade, the majority of asylum seekers from Central America and parts of Mexico are victims of torture, rape, incessant gang death threats, and extortion. They are prime targets for human trafficking. They come in fear. Indeed, scores of asylum seekers forced to return to their home countries by the US Government have been killed shortly after their return.

In 2013–14 and again in 2018–19, Brownsville saw an influx of Central American refugees far surpassing anything witnessed in the Dirty Wars era.[8] Fortunately, James and his friends and colleagues at the Good Neighbor Settlement House, Jack White and Marianela Ramírez Watson, were there to receive them, and to welcome them with dignity.

BUILDING BRIDGES IN A WORLD OF WALLS

James began giving back to the Brownsville community as a boy, emptying his pockets of nickels and dimes into the Methodist Episcopal Church offering each Sunday. As a youth, he was a regular participant in local relief and mission projects. In college at Southern Methodist University, he volunteered at the Methodist Settlement House, in deeply marginalized West Dallas, tutoring young people in English and coaching them in sports.

Little wonder that James eventually found his way to Yale Divinity School. He began his professional life as a pastor, ordained in the United Methodist Church in 1956.

Ministry took him to Montero, Bolivia. There, James lived and preached among a multicultural population of Spanish- and

---

8 Sieff, Kevin. "When Death Awaits Deported Asylum Seekers." *washingtonpost.com*, 26 Dec. 2018, www.washingtonpost.com/graphics/2018/world/when-death-awaits -deported-asylum-seekers.

Quechua-speaking people for nine years. He helped to develop the Rural Institute of Montero, an academic high school specializing in agriculture, which started with seven students and now educates over a thousand each year.

Also at this time, the United Methodist Church implemented a public health program in collaboration with Johns Hopkins University that went to battle with Montero's 32.4 percent infant mortality rate, which hit 0 percent in 2018. The population had grown from three thousand five hundred in James's day to one hundred fifty thousand when he last visited in 2016.

After a year as the executive secretary of the Methodist Church in Cochabamba, James left the ministry and moved his family of six to St. Louis, Missouri. There, he worked in the spirit of American social activist Saul Alinsky as a community organizer and director of political education for Teamsters Local Union 688. That was 1966.

In 1972, he returned home to Brownsville to help with the family businesses: a grocery store opened by his father, James Pace Sr., during the Great Depression; and his brother's fishing company. Fifteen years later, at the age of sixty-three, James went back to a first love, education, securing another advanced degree, this time as a teacher of English Literature and Grammar, and joining the Brownsville Independent School District (BISD), where his father once served as president of the Board.

But James Sr. wasn't the only pillar of Brownsville's community. Zenobia Gilmore Pace, James Jr.'s mother, was a lifelong Sister of Charity and the model for his faith. She coached women leaders of her local United Methodist Church Women's Society of Christian Service. She was also one of five Methodist women to found a settlement house in 1952.

Called The Good Neighbor Settlement House, its mission was to serve the local poor and homeless. By 2018, Good Neighbor was supporting the needs of asylum seekers as well—just like its historic counterpart.

INTRODUCTION

THE SETTLEMENT HOUSE TRADITION

As the nineteenth century tipped into the twentieth, Jane Addams and Ellen Gates Starr opened their Chicago home to immigrants.[9] They called their project Hull House and for several decades both leaders as well as residents of Hull House adapted and expanded to serve the needs of a diverse and ever-changing population. Their good work birthed the US Settlement House Movement.[10]

Responding to the challenges facing immigrants, especially undereducated women, they offered much more than charity: They built child care centers and schools; food banks and communal kitchens; shared laundry facilities and health clinics. They invited the participation of university scholars and local leaders, giving rise, as well, to the profession of Social Work.

By the 1920s, there were nearly five hundred Hull House–inspired facilities all over the country, serving not just immigrants but the indigent and less-abled. Zenobia Pace and her colleagues established Good Neighbor Settlement House on this model. Brownsville's Casa Romero followed suit, pivoting in the 1990s, when peace looked hopeful in Central America and refugee flows slowed, to become a "holistic Homeless Services Program" in a new location and under a new name: The Bishop E. San Pedro, Ozanam Center. In addition to delivering emergency shelter for refugees, both Ozanam and Good Neighbor continue to provide homeless prevention through case management as well as food pantry services to Brownsville's most vulnerable: poor families, runaway youth, the elderly, and those with substance abuse problems, mental illness, and other special needs.

---

9 Schatz, Kate. "The Women Who Welcomed Immigrants." yesmagazine.org, 27 Mar 2020, www.yesmagazine.org/social-justice/2020/03/27/women-welcomed-immigrants.

10 Scheuer, Jeffrey. "Origins of the Settlement House Movement," Excerpt from, *Legacy of Light: University Settlement's First Century*. New York: University Settlement, 1985 in VCU Libraries Social Welfare History Project https://socialwelfare.library.vcu.edu /settlement-houses/origins-of-the-settlement-house-movement.

SECURITY TRUMPS HUMANITY

Sadly, regional peace was fleeting. As the twentieth century gave way to the twenty-first, civil wars gave way to drug wars. Transnational drug-smuggling operations required gangs, which quickly birthed rival cartels, whose turf battles now menace civilian populations with ever-increasing impunity throughout Latin America and the Central American isthmus all the way to the two-thousand-mile US-Mexico border. In 2004, tending to the needs of two hundred refugees would have been considered a busy day for Rio Grande Valley humanitarians.[11] Fast-forward to 2014, and the borderlands saw those numbers double when roughly seventy thousand families and another seventy thousand unaccompanied children arrived at the border in a single year.[12]

This time, refugees were fleeing crippling poverty as well as gang violence and brutality. But the so-called "Drug Wars" had by then combined with a post-9/11 zeitgeist of fear, bringing a super-charged "law and order" approach to the borderlands. Barriers both seen and unseen were erected to "secure" US citizens from potential terrorist attacks. Border patrols were replaced with Border Patrol armadas, trained to believe all crossers guilty until proven innocent.

A newly militarized border threatened to render humanitarianism obsolete. It also made the trafficking of migrants a lucrative sideline for the criminal cartels, putting at ever-greater risk the world's most vulnerable people. Fortunately, as the drumbeat of division drove a stake into the heart of the borderlands, the call for a more compassionate response toward those in need beat more loudly as well.

---

11 Salgado, Soli and Dan Stockman. "Sr. Norma Pimentel, LCWR award recipient, embraces 'holy chaos' of her ministry to migrants." *globalsistersreport.org*, 17 Aug 2019, www.globalsistersreport.org/news/ministry-trends/sr-norma-pimentel-lcwr-award-recipient -embraces-holy-chaos-her-ministry.

12 Lind, Dara. "The 2014 Central American migrant crisis." *vox.com*, 10 Oct 2014, www.vox.com/2014/10/10/18088638/child-migrant-crisis-unaccompanied-alien-children -rio-grande-valley-obama-immigration.

INTRODUCTION

THE VIEW FROM GROUND ZERO

In the spring of 2018, the winds of change blew across the border again. That April, then-Attorney General Jeff Sessions announced "zero tolerance" for anyone who dared to cross into the US from the south. Marking all migrants—even asylum seekers—as criminals, the administration he served demanded they be treated that way.

Everyone was detained, even children, in ill-equipped processing centers meant to be temporary way stations, and for far longer than the legal three-day limit. Families were ripped apart, separated, and funneled into different bureaucratic purgatories.[13] And rather than deliver those who were released directly to area shelters and respite centers, as per Border Patrol practice to that point, Immigration and Customs Enforcement (ICE) agents simply loaded them into white buses and dumped them, penniless, hungry, filthy, and confused, at Rio Grande Valley bus stations.

It was a humanitarian crisis.

"Prior to their release and while in US custody," states James, "the migrants were thrust into cold storage detention (*la hielera*)[14] from one to twelve days, with inadequate food or clothing, intense light 24/7, and, at times, so crowded in they could only sleep standing up."

Sister Norma Pimentel, Executive Director of Catholic Charities RGV, was one of very few people outside the US Department of Homeland Security ever to be allowed a peek inside the now-infamous

---

13 Towle, Sarah. "Confronting the Cruelest Policy of All: Jodi Goodwin spearheads a legal triage effort to free parents from ICE and reunite them with their children kidnapped by Uncle Sam." *medium.com*, 23 Jul 2020, https://medium.com/the-first-solution /confronting-the-cruelest-policy-of-all-family-separation-a411fbbd08c7.

14 Towle, Sarah. Interview with James Pace, 6 July, 2021. These are the Customs and Border Protection (CBP) concrete holding cells colloquially known as "iceboxes" because of their dangerously low temperatures.

Ursula Processing Center in McAllen, Texas. "That experience has marked me forever," she remembers.[15]

She describes seeing close to one hundred children packed into cage-like cells, with no showers, few mats to sleep on, and no room to sit or lie down, in frigid temperatures, all crying and pulling on her dress, saying, *Please get me out of here.* The memory remains for her, "like a dagger in my heart."[16]

That's when she reached out to request the aid of other local sanctuaries and respite centers, like the Good Neighbor Settlement House, which she knew, in the right hands, was capable of scaling up to serve eight hundred people at a time.

"JACK, WE HAVE A PROBLEM."

"When Sister Norma asks you to do something," says Jack White, MSW, then Good Neighbor's volunteer director, "you jump, and ask how high later."

He recalls her sending him to the Brownsville bus station as the numbers of migrants landing in McAllen were reaching record highs of eight hundred to one thousand a day.[17] Sure enough, he found that ICE was dropping people in Brownsville as well, fifty at a time, hundreds a day, until as late as 9:00 p.m. Some were released directly from *la hielera* processing centers, still in the same filthy clothes they'd been wearing when they crossed the border. Others had been detained in prison-like conditions for months, in some cases without knowledge of the fate of their children and spouses.

"They were traumatized. They didn't know where they were going or how to get there. They had no money, no English, no direction,"

---

15 Catholic News Service. "Sister Pimentel shares stories from the border with US priests." Copyright © 2019 Catholic News Service, *cruxnow.com*, 13 Jul 2019, https://cruxnow.com /church-in-the-usa/2019/07/sister-pimentel-shares-stories-from-the-border-with-u-s-priests.
16 Ibid.
17 Ibid.

states Jack. "When the bus station closed at midnight, they were pushed outdoors to sleep on the surrounding streets."

Fortunately, according to James, Jack's particular genius is in raising armies of volunteers. Five years earlier, he prevented the Good Neighbor Settlement House from having to shutter its doors by increasing its volunteer workforce. In 2018, Good Neighbor's wheels were turning smoothly thanks to the efforts of three paid staff members and a cadre of volunteers that clocked in 1.5 million hours annually.

That summer, Jack and his volunteers became immediately enmeshed with Sergio Cordova, Michael Benavides, and Andrea Rudnik of the just-formed Team Brownsville,[18] a group of local educators that stepped up in the face of the crisis. They handed out travel packs previously stuffed with water, snacks, and other necessities, like diapers. They marked up US maps with migrants' ongoing travel itineraries; bought them meals and bus tickets; and taught them a few useful English phrases to help everyone on their way. For those whose buses were not leaving for hours or days, they ran a round-the-clock escort service to Good Neighbor, located just a few blocks away. There, staff and volunteers were moving nonstop, feeding people, outfitting them with new clothes, and bedding them down for the night after a warm shower.

"When Jack called me in September, asking me to help him with the refugee and asylee program at Good Neighbor, I immediately replied, *'Yes!'* recalls James. After fourteen years of teaching full-time and four more years of substitute teaching, James Pace retired at eighty-one. In the summer of 2018, at age eighty-seven, he commenced to waking up at 4:30 a.m., five mornings a week, to greet asylum seekers arriving at the Brownsville bus station from 5:30 a.m.

"James was the first person there every morning," says Jack.

---

18 Towle, Sarah. "Writing the Handbook for a More Humane World: What Five Texas Teachers Can Teach Global Leadership About Running a Refugee Camp and Containing COVID-19." medium.com, 19 May 2020, https://medium.com/the-first-solution/meet -the-dedicated-volunteers-writing-the-handbook-for-a-more-humane-world-f6e9dab2832b.

"We welcomed them with smiles, oriented them, loaned them our personal cell phones to call their friends and relatives with whom they were going to live."

That's also when Jack brought in another Brownsville native to aid the effort: Sister Marianela Ramírez Watson. She married into the Methodist Church in 1986 and has worked with United Methodist Women ever since. She served as president of the local chapter from 1990–93 and became district treasurer in early 2018. From September of that year, she could also be found first thing every morning at the Brownsville bus station. In addition to providing travel packs and bus routes, she also kept detailed records, becoming the primary public relations person and archivist of the humanitarian push-back against the Trump administration's immigration agenda of "deterrence by cruelty."

"It was an incredible time to be living and serving in Brownsville," says Jack. "It seemed the whole community turned out to help. My job was to open up everything possible at Good Neighbor to support the humanitarian mission, secure the help and buy-in of our municipal leadership, and to inspire volunteers to take action."

Still, the numbers of asylum seekers passing through the Rio Grande Valley were so high, Good Neighbor's team struggled to accommodate everyone. As Jack says, "The logistics of it all threatened to stretch our capacity at times."

NO REST FOR THE WEARY

Fortunately, in addition to Sister Norma's Humanitarian Respite Center, The Ozanam Center, Iglesia Bautista West Brownsville, and La Posada Providencia in nearby San Benito stepped up to offer overflow shelter when the Good Neighbor Settlement House hit capacity. The collective effort hummed from the summer of 2018 through the holidays. Then, one January evening at 5:00 p.m., Jack received his first-ever phone call from ICE.

"They don't usually direct communications to people like me," he says. But they wanted him to know that instead of dropping migrants off at the bus station throughout the day, as they had been, they would henceforth be delivering them directly to Good Neighbor Settlement House. He could expect two hundred to three hundred people the very next day . . . starting at 7:00 a.m.!

This gave Jack less than twelve hours to turn an operation staffed by three into a round-the-clock system. "It was then we went into madness.[19] What followed was expansion to a twenty-four hour, seven day a week service. We put bandaids over bandaids; our medical clinic was overwhelmed; showers broke down. We had to reconfigure food preparation to provide for both refugees as well as our homeless. We had to set up sleep spaces in spare rooms over the food bank and in the community room, where we packed in up to three hundred a night."

The local police chief called ICE to give them a piece of his mind for causing an untenable public safety crisis. But somehow the Brownsville humanitarian community managed, and the "holy chaos," as Sister Norma dubbed it, ticked along until July 2019. That's when the Trump administration erected the most impenetrable wall of all thus far: The Migrant "Protection" Protocols (MPP), which didn't protect anyone at all.

Rolled out in San Diego on January 24, 2019, and otherwise known as the "Remain in Mexico" program, MPP required asylum seekers to wait out, in some of the most dangerous places on Earth, the adjudication of their claims—decided in kangaroo courts[20] under border-hugging

---

19 Gonzalez, Valerie. "24 Hours at an Immigrant Shelter: Adaptation to Challenges." *krgv.com*, 2 Apr 2019, www.krgv.com/news/24-hours-at-an-immigrant-shelter-adaptation -to-challenges, © KRGV.
20 Kopan, Tal. "Exclusive: Outgoing SF immigration judge blasts courts as 'soul crushing,' too close to ICE." *San Francisco Chronicle*, 18 May 2021, https://www.sfchronicle .com/politics/article/Exclusive-Outgoing-SF-immigration-judge-blasts-16183235.php.

big-top tents over video conference calls with little legal representation and no language translation other than Spanish.[21]

It took six months for MPP to flow east with the Rio Grande. At which point, bus stations, respite centers, and shelters all over the Valley went shockingly, eerily quiet.

RECLAIMING THE HUMANITY OF THE BORDERLANDS

One early afternoon, before the implementation of MPP, a teenaged girl arrived at Good Neighborhood Settlement House. She carried an infant child in her arms. Sister Marianela reached out to give the girl a hug and to help lighten her load. But the young woman recoiled in panic. She cried out, "No, you can't take my baby!"

Marianela reassured her that she meant no harm. "You and your baby are among friends, here," she said.

Once the young mother had settled in and regained her composure, Marianela invited her to share her story. She learned that an immigration officer at the Gateway International Bridge, the US Port of Entry connecting Brownsville with Matamoros, Mexico, had tried to take the girl's child, not believing it was hers. And this happened just hours after the two had escaped an attempted kidnapping.

The young mother was clearly traumatized. And her story didn't even include what forced her to run in the first place. Marianela learned only that they had flown from Guerrero, Mexico, to Matamoros two days before.

"I felt good knowing I was only a few kilometers from the border with the US," the young mother recounted. She had hailed a taxi, asking the driver to take her to the bridge, but on exiting the airport, he turned south.

---

21 Transactional Records Access Clearinghouse at Syracuse University, "Details on MPP (Remain in Mexico) Deportation Proceedings, (Hearing Location=MPP Brownsville Gateway International Bridge)." *trac.syr.edu*, 22 Oct 2020, https://trac.syr.edu/phptools /immigration/mpp/about_data.html.

She knew it was not the right direction, and told him so. He replied, *"No, señora, vamos a Ciudad Victoria. No, ma'am, we're going to Ciudad Victoria."*

That was 320 kilometers away—the wrong way!

She demanded that he turn around and take her to Matamoros. When he didn't, she emptied her purse of all her remaining bills and coins—about one hundred dollars.

"I told him all of it was his, if he would just take me to the bridge leading to the US."

He did, fortunately. And the mother did not subsequently lose her child to overzealous Customs and Border Protection agents, like so many.

"But what of the numerous youngsters who don't have the resources for a bribe?" Marianela asks. "Are they condemned to be sex slaves?"

MOTHER OF EXILES

Stories such as this humanize the plight of migrants and refugees to the US. They call into question the labels, stereotypes, and myths used by anti-immigrant forces to justify such policies as family separation and MPP. To some, individuals like this young mother and her infant child are criminals and drug dealers coming for your jobs. They are "aliens" and "illegals" and "lazy cheaters," who failed to migrate "the right way"—not the resourceful fifteen-year-old potential victim of a sex crime, running away from her abuser and toward a better future.

That's what motivated James Pace to interview asylum seekers passing through the Good Neighbor Settlement House in the fall and winter of 2018 and 2019: to put a human face on the folks the Trump administration wanted to disappear into Mexico or fly back to certain harm; and to enlighten Americans beyond the borderlands as to what these people were fleeing.

"When I approach an asylum seeker," states James of his process, "I smile and say, 'Welcome brother, Welcome sister,' as I extend to them my hand. I tell them I wish to capture the stories of their experiences—in their homeland, on their journey north, and what happened to them on arrival at the border—in order to acquaint US citizens about what they've really been through. I tell them I have already interviewed many others from their countries of origin: Honduras, El Salvador, Guatemala, Nicaragua, as well as Cuba and parts of Mexico."

Inevitably, they'd settle in with James and speak their truth, in part because he exudes warmth and compassion; in part *because they want us to know* they are real people with hopes and dreams and beating hearts, seeking their human right to live without fear of persecution.

In the end, James captured over one hundred interviews, which he transcribed, translated, and titled himself. This compilation of eighty-five, organized in eight chapters, each introduced by biblical scripture, high-light centuries-old human cruelties as well as love's response. Together they represent how James Pace of Brownsville, Texas, endeavored to live his whole life long: according to the Gospel of Matthew 25:34–40.

'Come, you who are blessed by my Father . . .
For I was hungry and you gave me something to eat,
I was thirsty and you gave me something to drink,
I was a stranger and you invited me in,

I needed clothes and you clothed me . . .'
. . . The King will then say, 'I tell you the truth,
Whatever you did for one of the least of these
Brothers of mine, you did for me.'

INVITATION

In a recent conversation, James shared this pearl with me: "When I look into the eyes of a brother or sister asylum seeker, I see the love and mercy of Jesus."

I find that same love and mercy in these stories. I invite you to read and absorb these tales of hope, power, and resilience in the face of horror and extraordinary circumstances; to meet the double-sided coin that is humankind—capable of such darkness as well as such glorious kindness.

May they aid us in reclaiming the soul of our nation and of our borderlands. May they move us, one and all, to build back better with immigration practices established on structures of humanity and welcome.

We can do better. We must. And as the folks at the Good Neighbor Settlement House prove every day, we know how: with communities of caring rather than criminalization.

All it takes is the popular will to educate social workers and trauma specialists rather than Border Patrol agents and security guards; to create childcare rather than detention centers; to raise armies of volunteers to stock food banks and cook in communal kitchens. We must harness the participation of Church, University, and local political leaders, as Jane Addams did a century ago and as Jack did when Good Neighbor faced insolvency, to provide clinics and counselors dedicated to the physical and mental health needs of human beings, no matter the language they speak or on which side of an arbitrary borderline they happen to be born.

We must, at the very least, be guided, like James, by justice.

SARAH TOWLE

Educator, Historian, Human Rights Defender, and Author:
The First Solution: Tales of Humanity and Heroism from the US Borderlands
JUNE 2021

■ ■ ■

INTERVIEWS OF ASYLUM SEEKERS
AT THE GOOD NEIGHBOR SETTLEMENT HOUSE, BROWNSVILLE, TEXAS
2018–2019

Oral Histories conducted, translated, and written by
JAMES PACE

Chapter 1

FREEDOM

"To the Jews who had believed him, Jesus said, 'If you hold to my teaching, you are really my disciples. Then you will know the truth, and the truth will set you free.' They answered him, 'We are Abraham's descendants and have never been slaves of anyone. How can you say that we shall be set free?' Jesus replied, 'Very truly I tell you, everyone who sins is a slave to sin. Now a slave has no permanent place in the family, but a son belongs to it forever.'"

JOHN 8:31–36
New International Version (NIV) Bible

I'm Free! I'm Free!

It was the first week we were helping the asylum seekers coming to the US in September, 2018. Virginia White, Jack White, and I, Jim Pace, were sitting in the Brownsville, Texas, bus station at 5:30 a.m. awaiting the arrival of asylum seekers from the Port Isabel Detention Center. At that time, we did not know the director of the detention center ran it like a federal prison and the inmates were treated like felons.

Consequently, the asylum seekers on the bus had their hands shackled and their legs in leg irons. It required extra time to remove all the restraints, before they were released to us at the bus station, causing them to be fifteen to twenty minutes late.

Finally, the asylees came flooding through the station's entrance, and we welcomed them, getting them to line up at the ticket counter, letting them know we were volunteers ready to serve them. We loaned them our personal cell phones to call family and friends living in the US, helped them straighten out problems with their bus tickets, informed them they were in Brownsville, Texas, so they could reassure relatives and friends from their final destinations. We then gave them a backpack filled with a blanket, clothes, a personal hygiene kit, and a bottle of water, plus a plastic kit with nonperishable food for the bus trip.

Shortly before departure, some of the asylum seekers came to where Jack White and I were standing to say goodbye. A Cuban man faced Jack and shook hands while Jack told him, "Congratulations."

I noticed his eyes begin to moisten, and then when we shook hands, the Cuban began to cry and took a step backward. With tears falling down his cheeks, and a smile spreading across his face, he raised his arms and shouted,

"I'm free! I'm free!"

■   ■   ■

Words of Óscar Toobal Botzotz

Hello, my good Christian friends. I am a sixteen-year-old Guatemalan male just released from the Port Isabel, Texas, refugee detention center. My refugee friends and I refer to it as a detention center; the center's director calls it a prison. We were treated like prisoners, surrounded by two very high cyclone fences topped by razor-sharp triple strings of barbed wire; confined for periods in a very cold chamber for violating rules of conduct; enduring a sleepless night, without even a cup of coffee or cold tortilla before being dropped off at the Brownsville bus station; manacled and shackled on the trip from the detention center to the bus station.

Yet, I am so happy, despite having been jailed for two years and four months. I am free, among new friends who welcome me with smiles. 'We are here to help you; we can provide you with a backpack filled with food and hygiene items, clothes and a blanket for the cold of the bus, help in taking the necessary steps to obtain your bus ticket, free use of our personal cell phones to call your relatives at your destination, and a refuge where you can rest, eat, shower for a few hours, or remain overnight to travel tomorrow.'

I am so happy. I'm free. I'm smiling and laughing constantly. I want to sing and dance. I'm going to live with my brother in New York whom I haven't seen in four years. I know I have to improve my English which I began to learn these past two years. But, I'm good at languages: fluent in Spanish, and two indigenous languages I learned in my beloved Guatemala.

I want to become a US citizen. I can't go back to Guatemala where there's so much corruption and the threat of death, if you don't join a gang.

You asked me, friend, what my dreams are. Someday I'm going to have a wife and children. They'll be proud of their *papi*. I'm going to be a social worker, specializing in working with children.

      ■   ■   ■

Today I Received Asylum

I am Luís Cortez, twenty-four years old, from Puerto Cortés, Honduras, with a university degree in accounting. Today, February 13, 2020, I received asylum from a US immigration court judge. I am so happy, just thrilled!

However, the cost was high. My family suffered the loss of seven members killed by the *pandillas* (gangs): my father, four uncles, and two teenaged cousins. It's no wonder Honduras has the reputation of being the most violent country in Central America. Our family's fate was caused by politics and wanting to help the little people of our country. The truth is that the drug cartels rule Honduras, not the government.

Realizing that I was next in line to be *fichado* (targeted) by the *pandillas* (gangs), I left my country by bus on July 30, 2019. Without warning or cause, I was detained and put in the city jail in Villahermosa, Mexico. After eight days in detention, I bribed a guard and escaped. On August 13th, I reached Reynosa, Mexico, and immediately crossed the Rio Grande to Texas in a *balsa* (inflatable raft) without having to pay one cent. I was taken by the *migra* (border patrol, slang) to the Hidalgo detention center for one day, and then returned to Matamoros, Mexico, where I would be marooned for six months in the tent city erected for asylum seekers. There I was helped and encouraged by the volunteers of *Team Brownsville*, led by Sergio Cordova.

Early today, February 13th, an unforgettable day, I crossed the bridge [to Brownsville, Texas] and went straight into a tent where federal court was being held for some twenty asylum seekers with an immigration judge via a video connection to communicate with us. When the judge

9

reviewed my documents and testimony, he immediately granted me asylum, signifying legal residence in the US.

So here I am at Good Neighbor Settlement House. When you ask me how I received asylum so quickly, it was because I had official documents and newspaper accounts of the seven assassinations in my family. Tonight I'm taking a Greyhound bus to Orlando, Florida, where I'll live with my brother and pursue my career in accounting.

■   ■   ■

In the US—In Spite of Its Policy

My name is Edwin Vivas, thirty-seven years old, with nine years of schooling in San Salvador, El Salvador. I was a telephone and internet technician from 2007–2019. I am a witness to the assassination of my best friend. I knew the killers would come for me, before I could identify them to the authorities. I had to leave El Salvador.

I took a bus heading to the US on June 21, 2019. I paid US$2,000 to a *coyote* (smuggler) for an uneventful trip, and reached Reynosa, Mexico, on June 30th. For twenty days, I stayed in a stash house, *Casa Díaz Ordaz*, and then crossed the Rio Grande in a *balsa* (inflatable raft) with the same *coyote* from the bus trip. The *migra* (border patrol) picked us up after the *coyote* called them on his cell phone to come detain us.

The *migra* took us to their headquarters in McAllen, Texas, on July 11th, where we spent six days in the *hielera* (cold storage detention room), without adequate clothing. It was so crowded we had to try to sleep standing up . . . and for six days!

Finally, we were transferred to El Valle Detention Facility in Raymondville, Texas; I remained there for six-and-a-half months. With so much free time on my hands and time to think, I came to realize I was in the US in spite of current government policy. Being from El Salvador, I had to first pass through Guatemala and Mexico, both countries which offered asylum to immigrants. US policy denied entrance to those who first passed through countries offering asylum. Lucky me! Some official did not apply the policy to me.

Early on the morning of February 5th, we left the detention center, were processed through the Brownsville bus station, and are now in the Good Neighbor Settlement House. Tonight I leave on a Greyhound bus to San Francisco, California, to live with my brother. After getting the proper papers, I hope to continue my career started in San Salvador.

■   ■   ■

Chapter 2

GOVERNMENT CONTROL

"Pilate called together the chief priests, the rulers and the people, and said to them, 'You brought me this man as one who was inciting the people to rebellion. I have examined him in your presence and have found no basis for your charges against him. Neither has Herod, for he sent him back to us; as you can see, he has done nothing to deserve death.

Therefore, I will punish him and then release him.' But the whole crowd shouted, 'Away with this man! Release Barabbas to us!' (Barabbas had been thrown into prison for an insurrection in the city, and for murder.)

Wanting to release Jesus, Pilate appealed to them again. But they kept shouting, 'Crucify him! Crucify him!'

For the third time he spoke to them: 'Why? What crime has this man committed? I have found in him no grounds for the death penalty. Therefore I will have him punished and then release him.' But with loud shouts they insistently demanded that he be crucified, and their shouts prevailed. So Pilate decided to grant their demand.

He released the man who had been thrown into prison for insurrection and murder, the one they asked for, and surrendered Jesus to their will."

LUKE 23:13–25
New International Version (NIV) Bible

THE FLIGHT INTO EGYPT
El Greco (Domenikos Theotokopoulos)
Candia, Crete (Greece), 1541 - Toledo (Spain), 1614
Ca. 1570. Oil on pine panel, Museo Nacional del Prado, Madrid

The Gospel of Saint Matthew succinctly narrates this episode: When they had gone, an angel of the Lord appeared to Joseph in a dream. "Get up", he said, "take the child and his mother and escape to Egypt. Stay there until I tell you, for Herod is going to search for the child to kill him." So he got up, took the child and his mother during the night and left for Egypt (Matthew 2:13–14).

■ ■ ■

Encountering Beasts on the Road

My small Nicaraguan community is very poor: no electricity, no running water, a rocky path for a main street which no cars are able to traverse, and a one-hour walk to reach a bus. I am a thirty-four-year-old illiterate farmer growing beans and corn with my brothers. Our farm is four acres. My father can't farm anymore because of bad kidneys. My pseudonym is Hernán Gómez.

Our government is very corrupt at all levels. What have they ever done for us? Our family bought a motorbike for me, and within four days, the authorities had confiscated it. It's no wonder there are protests against the government. My younger brother, twenty-eight years old, was shot in the head by police for marching with an anti-government sign held high. With his death, I knew I had to leave, or I would be next in the family to die. I would rather die on the road than at home.

My sister made contact with a *coyote* (smuggler) in the state of Tabasco, Mexico, and I paid him US$4,000 to get me through Mexico. Along with others, I took a bus to Tampico, and then on to Reynosa, Mexico, opposite McAllen, Texas. Arriving in Reynosa at 4:00 a.m., a man in the bus station approached me and said he would help me get across the border. He took me to a stash house for refugees, and there were three companions already there. I was thrust into a horrible, gruesome, and life-threatening situation. The gang members had cut off two fingers of each of the three men, photographed them after the amputation, and sent photos of each man demanding ransom of US$35,000 for each, or else. I really got scared about my fate; so when they asked me how much money I had, I immediately told them and handed over US$2000, not telling them I had US$500 hidden in my shoe.

When they found out about my home in Nicaragua, I guess they lost interest in me, and let me go, giving me a *clave* (safe conduct code) to cross to the US. I went to the riverbank, and the woman in charge of several launches asked me if I had a *clave*. I showed her mine, paid her US$200 and crossed with several others and a *coyote* (smuggler) in a launch. There were six of us. The *coyote* took us to the outskirts of McAllen, and gave us a map to get to a safe house in McAllen. We made it to the safe house, but later the same day the *migra* (border patrol) raided it, handcuffed us, took us somewhere, and put us in the *hielera* (cold storage detention room) for ten days. From there, we were taken to El Valle Detention Facility in Raymondville, Texas, and I was detained for seventy-five days.

So here I am at Good Neighbor Settlement House on March 9th. I am going to live with my brother in Los Angeles, California, who is undocumented, like thousands in the same situation. In just a month, on April 10th, I will have my hearing with the immigration court judge to decide if I can stay in the US.

One thing I know—I am NOT going back. I've spent too much time and money to get here. My future is here in the US. To send me back to Nicaragua is to send me back to die.

■　　■　　■

Just a Private

For two years, I was just a private in the Honduran army. I'm twenty years old with a seventh-grade education. My family consists of my mother and a nine-year-old brother living in the mountains of Comayagua, Honduras.

It's threatening to be a soldier in today's Honduras. While you're fighting the *pandillas* (gangs) and *narcotraficantes* (drug traffickers) every day, there's no support from either the politicians or the local police. They're all corrupt; bought out by the very people we are fighting. You're also ordered to stop all public protests against the government. One afternoon we had to disperse some protesters marching in a parade. We had to start fighting them, really mixing it up. I took several hard blows. Then when we turned them around and they retreated, they started throwing hand-sized rocks at us. One couldn't dodge all of them, for the protesters were throwing rocks in volleys. Suddenly, I felt a blow to my knee. I fell to the ground and couldn't get up. Man, how it hurt! Two of my comrades lifted me up, but I couldn't walk. My buddies carried me between them like I was a football player being carried off the playing field.

For four months, I couldn't walk. It still hurts me, even after more than a year. Meanwhile, I was discharged from the army and on January 8th, I left Honduras. I had a problem in Mexico with the drug cartels; they robbed me of all my money. I fled from them, got to the Rio Grande, and paid US$15.00 to cross the river in a launch. I spent a month in El Valle Detention Facility in Raymondville, Texas. Different from many other detainees, I felt my month there went well. Maybe that was because of my having been a soldier. I'm anxious to get going on my trip to live with my twenty-three-year-old brother in New York. My opinion about ICE [US Immigration and Customs Enforcement]? I have none. After all, I'm just a private.

■　■　■

Kill Us All?

I am an eighteen-year-old Guatemalan youth with one completed year of university studies in engineering. My pseudonym is Freddie Mengado. My mother and five of her children are already living in California, including a twenty-two-year-old sister, and four younger brothers. My dad is separated from my mother, and remains in Guatemala.

I had an aunt who was a political activist and university student worker. She reached a lot of students. At one student meeting, the police burst into the meeting hall, and shot and killed her while she was standing at the speaker's podium. I was a member of her student group, and as her relative, I knew I would be on the police's hit list. Therefore, I quickly left Guatemala for the US.

Once I get to California and reunite with my family, I'm going to enroll in a university for my second year of engineering studies. I've heard there's a scarcity of engineers here in the US, so I feel fortunate to have chosen engineering as my vocation. I will certainly remain in the US.

As I reflect on my life in Guatemala, I am ready to shout out, "The police can't kill us all."

■ ■ ■

Message Not Received

(interview contributed by Andrea Rudnik,
Team Brownsville)

The first thing you notice about Omar is he is missing his index finger on his right hand. It's not the kind of thing I wanted to ask about, not right away anyway. But Omar doesn't hold back. Speaking softly in Spanish, he begins to tell me his story right away.

'They tried to kill me. They tried to make me join their gang, but I didn't want to. I have five kids and a wife. I tried to be a good father, a good provider for my family, but they came after me.'

He told me that his city of Puerto Cortés, Honduras, had changed a lot in the last ten years. Puerto Cortés had been a small city, away from the danger of San Pedro Sula and the capital, Tegucigalpa. That's where the gangs used to be the strongest. Puerto Cortés was out of the way, up on the north coast.

But now, everything was different. The gangs had a stronghold there. The drugs and weapons were everywhere. If you didn't join, you were fair game to be attacked and killed. So they came after him. They wanted him to join, but he was a Christian. He didn't want any part of it.

One night last December, members from the Mara Salvatrucha [MS-13] gang attacked him and nearly killed him. They slashed his body eighteen times with a machete, including around his neck and face. They cut off his index finger to send a message: join the gang or die. But for Omar, it was a message not received. He had his faith in Jesus Christ above all, and after many days in the hospital, he was finally released. He knew he had to leave Puerto Cortés, escape with his life, and try to get to the United States. He knew enough about going to the United States that he thought he had a good case for political asylum. Maybe then he could bring his family. It was the only thing on his mind, as he made the perilous trip through Guatemala, Mexico, and then across the river near Reynosa.

He didn't know he would spend four months in detention; that he'd be thrown into the *hielera* (cold storage detention room) for days; that they would accuse him of lying, even with all his scars and a missing finger; that they would threaten to deport him. He didn't know he would have to remove his shirt in front of the judge to show all of the machete marks on his neck and back. But in the end, the judge believed him, believed he had a credible fear of persecution. And so, he was released *bajo palabra*, on his own recognizance, without bond.

He says he credits everything, every success he's had in the United States, to his faith. He didn't know how he was going to come up with bail money, and then he didn't have to. He didn't know where he would stay when he was released, and then Casa xxx, an immigrant shelter in xxx, came through for him.

He didn't know *Team Brownsville*/Good Neighbor Settlement House would be there at the bus station to help him get his ticket straightened out, and make sure the shelter knew he was coming. He didn't know we would give him a backpack with a blanket, pillow, and a new Bible. He didn't know there were people that would care so much about his well-being. He didn't know that we want to know what happens next for him, that we want to help him get his family here, too, if possible.

Omar left with a real message received today. He left knowing Americans do care about his safety and welfare. He left knowing that even though we didn't know him on entering the bus station, we cared about him enough to listen to his story and believe he was telling the truth. He blessed us with his presence, and blessed all of us with his words, before he left. Welcome to the United States!

■　　■　　■

Cattle Buyer to Brick Mason

My name is Marlon M. Cruz, a forty-seven-year-old Nicaraguan with no formal education. Buying and selling cattle for a brief time in Costa Rica, but mainly in Nicaragua, I've supported my wife and five sons all these years. I'm accustomed to large families; my mother had six daughters and three sons.

For nearly forty-seven years, I lived in peace . . . no problems. Then I started helping the students in their protests by transporting them in my truck to their meetings and marches on three occasions, some ten to twelve kilometers to a neighboring province.

That's when the black-shirted soldiers stepped in and changed my life on July 20, 2019, when the march ended. There had been growing opposition to the government for the past twenty to twenty-five years. During that time, I had stayed in the countryside on farms and ranches. Now it was, "Leave here or ?" I sought advice from an uncle, and he told me, "Get out of here; I'll help you."

I left Nicaragua by bus on December 5, 2018. When I got to Camargo, Mexico, the Mexican authorities left me *de yesca* (left me dry, penniless), and it was only through the aid of a cousin already in the US that I could continue my trip. By January 5th, I was in McAllen, Texas, detained by the *migra* (border patrol). I spent seven days in *la hielera* (cold storage detention room), followed by seventy-three days combined in the Raymondville and Port Isabel, Texas, detention centers. The food and treatment was good. Now I'm on my way to Miami where I plan to get into construction and become a brick mason.

■ ■ ■

A "Gusano"

For the last ten years, the Cuban Communist government has considered me a *gusano* (literally, "worm"; in Cuba, "counter-revolutionary"). I never was jailed for my political views, but I was clubbed and beaten in protest marches, and for attending supposedly clandestine political meetings during my last ten years in Cuba. After the last beating, on March 29, 2019, I left Cuba for Nicaragua.

My name is Alfredo García Hernández, a metal salesman (steel, copper, aluminum), fifty-two years old, the eldest of five brothers living in the city of Ciego de Ávila. I have a high school education. Cuba and Nicaragua are friendly politically and economically, so I had no trouble getting a passport and visa to fly to Nicaragua to buy clothing and a few household items. On April 10, 2019, I left Nicaragua by bus to come to the US. After a trip without complications, I crossed the bridge from Reynosa, Mexico, to Hidalgo, Texas, where I was picked up by the *migra* (border patrol), and taken to their headquarters on June 2nd. There I was put in the *hielera* (cold storage detention room) with its severe cold, 24/7 intense glaring light, and three small corn tacos as our daily food. After seven days in the *hielera*, I next went to El Valle Detention Facility in Raymondville, Texas. I was there for two months; the staff treatment and food were both good, even though I had to spend another two days in the *hielera*, both upon arrival and departure.

Now I'm here at the Good Neighbor Settlement House in Brownsville, ready to make the short hop of one-hundred-fifty miles to Corpus Christi, Texas, where I'll live with my thirty-one-year-old son, and my twenty-eight-year-old daughter. I'll take whatever job I can find. Perhaps in an oil refinery?

■　■　■

Sandino Walker

I am a thirty-eight-year-old father of three daughters from Matagalpa, Nicaragua. My daughters are Katarina, fourteen, Karen, twelve, and Karoulka, nine. The agricultural products in my area of northern Nicaragua are coffee, cacao, beans, corn, and cattle. I am a cattle buyer, buying creole cattle from ranchers and selling them to the slaughterhouses. I come from a large family with seven brothers, all of whom work in some specialty of the cattle business.

I have come to the US because of my fear of death. I entered the political arena to help the elderly and students in their protests against the Ortega government. The elderly represent 7 percent of the national population and had their $85.00 monthly subsidy reduced by 5 percent, while the price of beans was increased by nearly 400 percent. There is no free commerce in today's Nicaragua; it is all controlled by the government, with a great deal of the government "take" going into Ortega's pockets. After twelve years in power, President Ortega is a multimillionaire . . . and the working man? . . . ever increasing poverty. So I joined the elderly, students, and priests who marched with us and offered sanctuary within the churches. At the same time, the police and self-appointed militia increased their tactics and firepower against us. I was shot at more than I want to remember. Finally, I told my family that I either had to flee to the US or get killed.

I took a bus to Mexico. A *coyote* (smuggler) carried me in a truck through Mexico for US$3,500; then, I paid US$1,000 to be crossed north of McAllen, Texas. I was picked up by the border patrol and thrown in the *hielera* (cold storage detention room) for eight days, sleeping on a thin piece of plastic on the floor without a blanket, and eating cold and often stale baloney sandwiches the entire eight days. I had to wait to get much needed medicine when I was transferred to the detention center in Raymondville, Texas, for forty-five days, and then another forty-five days in the detention center of Port Isabel, Texas. To answer your question about my treatment while in the detention centers, it wasn't too bad.

I bonded out of the detention center with a US$12,500 bond, paying 10 percent in cash. I'll be staying with a friend in Los Angeles. I hope to get a job quickly, even though I know that endangers my status here in the US. Hopefully, I can get some job I already know in the cattle industry, and start sending money home to help support my family. I prefer to return to live some day in Nicaragua, but I am not too optimistic. Along with the general population, I have no confidence in the present Nicaraguan political parties. Some day democracy, justice, and liberty will come from the people, not the present parties. In the meantime, I can only work, pray, and hope.

■   ■   ■

Marching Together

I am a nineteen-year-old Nicaraguan youth; my pseudonym is Jaime Paz. My father worked in roof construction and repair in the city of Estelí, Nicaragua. I helped my dad from an early age, carrying his noon lunch to him. At thirteen, I began to help him on the job, culminating in an apprenticeship at eighteen. But, on April 19, 2018, my life changed. The protests of the elderly and students began.

I joined the protests in Estelí on April 23rd. At first, there were some three hundred students marching with the elderly. I was surprised to see gray-haired priests, as well as young priests marching. They declared the churches sanctuaries, but the police paid no heed; they entered the churches and dragged the protesters out. Our numbers swelled, and by my seventh and last march, we had grown to at least some five thousand marchers. There was a wonderful spirit. We were unified, together, young and old, raising our voices and putting our bodies on the line in our demand for justice and liberty. Many of us paid the price.

The combined forces of police, militia, and army clubbed us, shot some to death, shot rubber bullets, causing some protestors to lose an eye, and then there was always the tear gas. At the beginning of a march, there was both apprehension of what was to come and just plain fear. But then, with locked arms, singing and shouting, you began to march, and the fear disappeared.

I began to realize my personal situation was becoming very dangerous. I was identified as being an active leader in the marches. A police officer told me I was *fichado* (targeted) for death. After telling my dad, I boarded a bus on the outskirts of town, and traveled by bus through

Central America, Mexico, and came across the bridge to Brownsville, Texas, after waiting only two days to cross. I was only in the *hielera* (cold storage detention room) one day, then the Port Isabel Detention Center for thirty-five days. Now I'll be off to Miami today to join my uncle as a roofer.

I have no idea when I can return to Nicaragua. The army is solidly behind President Ortega. The only hope is that some day the people will rise up to produce a new Nicaragua. When will that be? *Quién sabe?* Who knows?

■　■　■

Three Jobs Not Enough

My name is Néstor Muñoz Olivera, forty-six years old, from Camagüey, Cuba, a city of some three hundred thousand inhabitants. I lived with my wife, mother, and younger sister, finishing the ninth grade of school. The cost of living is so high in Cuba that I took on three jobs—namely, construction, tire recapping, and being a chauffeur. Even with three jobs, I could not sustain my mother, sister, and me. My leaving Cuba had no political basis; it was strictly to have a better life earning more money for me and my wife.

I left Cuba on March 13, 2019; my wife had left a month earlier. I flew to Panama with a visa, supposedly to buy clothes and enjoy a week of tourism. I went by auto all the way through Central America and Mexico. I spent a week in Costa Rica to get a safe passage visa which cost me US$1,000. On May 12th, I arrived to Reynosa, Mexico, and immediately went to an evangelical church, *El Sendero de la Vida* (The Path of Life). Here I stayed sixty-three days. Previously, my wife had only stayed thirty days. I swam across the Rio Grande; I didn't pay one cent to cross into the US.

On July 15th, the *migra* (border patrol) took me to La Paloma, Texas, immigrant holding center where I stayed for nine days. Then I was transferred to the Coastal Bend Detention Center in Robstown, Texas, where I remained until August 27th. From there, they transported me to the Port Isabel Detention Center. You ask me to compare living at the two detention centers? No comparison. Coastal Bend has eight men in a room; Port Isabel has one hundred in a cage.

I left the Port Isabel Detention Center on August 28th, passed through the Brownsville bus station, and then here to Good Neighbor Settlement House. I'll stay here until I leave by bus at 10:00 p.m. for Las Vegas. I'll try to get a job as a truck driver. I know the pay and benefits will be better if I join the Teamsters Union.

■　■　■

Sendero de la Vida

(Path of Life)

I am a married thirty-eight-year-old Venezuelan named Gabriel Hernández Casanova. I attended the Monseñor de Talavera University & College in Caracas, with a degree in physical sciences, and a major in oceanography in 2007. Upon graduating, I went to work for a private company and became the director of various houses of medicine.

I joined the street protests against the government of President Maduro whose attitude was, "If you're not with me, you're my enemy." After the last two times in the street protests, I was accosted by the army captain in charge of the hospital where I worked. He threatened me and put a gun directly in my face. He repeated the same action against my wife. So we left Venezuela for Colombia on March 20, 2018.

We stayed in Colombia for a year, where I was threatened again by Venezuelan agents operating in Colombia. Consequently, we flew to Cancún, Mexico, and then again by plane to Monterrey. From there, we traveled by auto to Reynosa, Mexico, arriving May 2, 2019. We sought refuge in an evangelical church, *El Sendero de la Vida* (The Path of Life). My wife only stayed there one month before she crossed the Rio Grande to Hidalgo, Texas. I had to remain there three months, and followed her on July 29th to Hidalgo. I was taken to the headquarters of the *migra* (border patrol) where I had to endure the cold and inhumaneness of the *hielera* (cold storage detention room) for two days. On July 31st, I was transferred to the Coastal Bend Detention Center in Robstown,

Texas. The treatment was good, but I was then transferred to the Port Isabel Detention Center.

Wow! How surprised I was to experience the contrast between the detention centers in Robstown and Port Isabel! Port Isabel was a prison, and the inmates had heard the rumor the director was quoted as saying, "This is a prison, and I'm going to run it as a prison." I was released from the Port Isabel Detention Center today, October 26th, after a breakfast of a cold, stale baloney sandwich. I'll be leaving tonight from the Good Neighbor Settlement House here in Brownsville, Texas, for New Orleans, Louisiana, where I'll be reunited with my wife, who now lives with my brother-in-law. I'll wait until I'm eligible to work, and then I'll take whatever job I can find.

■   ■   ■

Industrial Engineer

My name is Marcos González, a fifty-year-old industrial engineer from Venezuela. My wife and two sons are already in Miami, Florida. I was a university professor for twelve years, specializing in the petroleum industry.

I became head of the engineering department, and voiced my opposition to the government and its two most recent presidents. I didn't like the government policies, and accused the two presidents of being criminals for tolerating or being involved directly in drug trafficking [*Cartel de los Soles*/Cartel of the Suns]. I feel lucky I was detained for only one year, but when freed, I knew I had to leave Venezuela.

I left for Colombia on July 1, 2019. I then took a plane to Monterrey, Mexico, and from there, a bus to Reynosa, Mexico, on July 4th. I crossed the Rio Grande by bus to McAllen, Texas, on July 31st. From there, I was taken by the US Border Patrol to the Port Isabel Detention Center, where I was detained for seventy-five days. I was released today, October 16th at 4:30 a.m., without any breakfast or even a cup of coffee. In fifteen minutes, the Brownsville police will take me from here, the Good Neighbor Settlement House, to the Brownsville/South Padre Island International Airport. I'll fly to Miami, Florida, to live with my family. First, I'll get a larger apartment for my family, and then I'll start looking for a university teaching job.

■　■　■

One-Thousand-One-Hundred Pounds
of Chicken

I am a forty-seven-year-old Cuban from *Isla de la Juventud* (Island of Youth) off the southern coast of Cuba. My name is Ramón Santesteban, with a wife and three sons still in Cuba. I am a university graduate with a degree in accounting.

Never agreeing with the government, since high school I have had to be careful expressing my political opinions. After working as an accountant for years, I became the director of a community center whose activities included selling foodstuffs at low prices that the working class could afford to buy. One day I advertised 500 kilos (1,100 pounds) of chicken. The same day the advertisement came out in our local newspaper, the local police entered the center, confiscated all of the chicken, accused me of being a *gusano* (counter-revolutionary), and detained me for seventy-two hours. The irony is that the authorities wanted to resell the chicken at a much higher price, while my price was true to the Cuban Revolution, with a price for the working man.

I knew that once being marked as a *gusano* in Cuba, I had no future in my country. I sold my home, paid a bribe of US$4,000 for a visa and US$2,500 for airfare to Cancún, and on to Reynosa, Mexico. I left Cuba on May 27, 2019, and then had to wait in Reynosa until July 24th, when I crossed the Rio Grande by bus to Hidalgo, Texas. I then was taken to El Valle Detention Facility in Raymondville, Texas.

I was later delivered to the Brownsville, Texas, bus station, and here I am with you at the Good Neighbor Settlement House.

I'm going by bus this afternoon to live with my brother in Florida. My brother has already lined up a job for me as a bookkeeper in a prosperous restaurant. I want to bring my wife and sons to the US as soon as possible.

■   ■   ■

They Were Shooting Women and Children

My pseudonym is Benito Juárez, a thirty-seven-year-old Nicaraguan. I come from the capital city, Managua, where I live with my wife, Ave María Mayorga, a lawyer. In contrast to my wife, I only finished the 10th grade of high school. My favorite subject was mathematics. I have worked as a taxi driver most of my life.

On April 19, 2018, the Sandinista government issued an edict reducing the social benefits of the elderly by 8 percent. They immediately began a protest march the next day, and were assaulted by the police. University students and then the general public joined the march of the old folks, and soldiers joined the police against the people. I joined by using my vehicle to take the protesters to the march's starting points, and ferrying the wounded protesters back to the hospitals.

Five weeks later, on May 30th, the Mother's Day March with women and children was held. The police and soldiers shot and massacred dozens of women and children—a horrible scene I will never forget. By then, I was *fichado como un gusano* (identified as a traitor) and, consequently, jailed. I was beat up, knocked to the floor, struck with a revolver above my eyebrow which required three stitches, kicked and hit with a baseball bat while lying on the floor. My wife saved me from being killed, by running to the United Nations Commission on Human Rights. She got a cease-and-desist order to end the torture. After two days, I was released from jail.

President Ortega and his wife and vice president, Rosario Murillo, lead a government with a terrible human rights record. During his presidency, approximately three thousand citizens have disappeared and one thousand seven hundred have been killed. In my opinion, Ortega is worse than Fidel Castro of Cuba. During all of this, Ortega has become a multimillionaire, and his son is following him with just a paltry half million. The father even had the triple crown world boxing champion, Alexis Argüello, killed in 2009, along with his wife, because the tyrant was afraid they were becoming the leaders of the Nicaraguan opposition. [Newspaper reports claim he died by suicide: a gunshot wound to the chest].

On June 23, 2019, I left Managua, walking first to a bus station on the outskirts of the city to avoid being spotted by the police. Without stopping, I went straight through El Salvador, Honduras, Guatemala, and Mexico, arriving in Reynosa, Mexico, on July 3rd. I had considered living in Costa Rica, so that my wife and son could join me quickly. However, several members of the United Nations Human Rights staff advised me to shun Costa Rica because [President] Ortega was sending in his agents dressed as civilians. They had killed a good number of Nicaraguans after tracking them down.

After staying in Reynosa two weeks, on July 17th I crossed the Rio Grande in a *balsa* (inflatable raft) with eight other asylum seekers. It cost each of us US$1,000.

I was detained by the *migra* (border patrol), taken to the *corral* (holding pen) in McAllen, Texas, where I spent eight days in the *hielera* (cold storage detention room), suffering from the cold, intense light 24/7, stale sandwiches, and sleeping standing up because the *hielera* was so crowded. Welcome to America, Benito! From there, I was taken to the Port Isabel Detention Center where I was treated well, and had the privilege of preaching the Gospel every day, and sometimes twice daily.

I'm going to Los Angeles, California, at six this evening to live with a family friend. As soon as I get to LA, I must get in touch with a priest I know to get my wife and son out of Nicaragua. Every day or two, a police car pulls up in front of my house, and the policeman asks my ten-year-old son, "Where's your *papi* (father)?" My son answers, "I don't know." If my wife is there, the same question and the same answer.

I know in my heart that my Lord and Savior Jesus Christ saved me from death, has been with me on my journey, and will be with me in my future life in California. I promised Jesus that I would always be faithful to Him, if He would get me to the US.

■　　■　　■

Seventeenth-Century Transport

On June 12, 2018, six *compañeros* (companions) slipped out of Cuba on a moonless night . . . destination? The Caribbean coast of Honduras. We were crammed into a 5.5-meter by 2-meter sailboat. Would you believe we cooked our own food on board? We ate vegetables and plentiful fish which we caught on our fifteen-day trip. We even had our prized *cafecitos* (demitasse cups of coffee). So when we got stuck on the reef protecting the island of Roatán, Honduras, on June 26th, all of us were in good physical shape.

All six of us had been identified by the Cuban government as *gusanos* (counter-revolutionaries), traitors to the Cuban Revolution. Since 1992, I had worked for five years as an industrial designer for the recovery of machine parts in a government-owned endeavor that had been established in response to the US blockade. That job paid me the equivalent of US$12.00 per month. For better pay, I began working as a brick mason for US$60.00 per month.

My life changed when I began to express publicly my political opinions by joining the *Movimiento Opositores por una Nueva República* (Opposition Movement for a New Republic) in 2015. I never went to prison, but I was detained and questioned for twelve days, and I knew what my future life would certainly become—prison or death. I began to plan to escape with my *compañeros*. We decided to build our own boat. Once built, it took us a day and a half to move it to the sea coast. You know the rest of the story in reaching Honduras.

The Honduran officials were very helpful. They transported us from the coast to the capital, Tegucigalpa, placed us in a shelter for immigrants, and then a TV station took over our story and published it along with a picture of "Six Undocumented Cuban Nationals Are Detained in Honduras." Then on to Nicaragua where we were detained for fifteen days; in Guatemala, the officials hit us up for $50 Quetzals (US$7.00). I stopped in Tapachula, Mexico, and worked for forty-five days as a brick mason for $300 Mexican Pesos per day (US$16.25). On arriving to Matamoros, Mexico, I stayed at an immigrant shelter for sixteen days, and then was eligible to cross the Rio Grande by bridge. I only had to endure the *hielera* (cold storage detention room) for one day. Then I was sent to El Valle Detention Facility in Raymondville, Texas, for forty days. Finally, I was transferred to the Port Isabel Detention Center for another three-and-a-half months. Now I'm off to Las Vegas to stay with my uncle who is partially paralyzed and has a few rental apartments. I've always wanted to be a professional truck driver. I'll start out by making local deliveries, and then move on to long-haul sixteen wheelers. I'll also be working to bring my two daughters, ages five and sixteen, to the US.

Before I quit talking, I want to make some observations about Cuba. You have a brain drain and working class exodus from Cuba, including middle-class professionals, doctors, nurses, engineers, etc. They are settling in many countries throughout Latin America, Mexico, and the US. I'll be thinking about the implications of this torrent of Cuban citizens turning their backs on the *patria* (homeland) during my two-day bus trip to Vegas. I want your opinion also, Jaime Pace; let's stay in touch.

■　■　■

Politics Push to US

My pseudonym is Muhammad D. Abul Abul, a thirty-two-year-old from Bangladesh. I speak Bengali and English. My wife is twenty-three-year-old Muschumi, and daughters Afsana, seven, Asmai, two, and son Nasmul, three months. I left Bangladesh on July 12, 2018. I first flew to Dubai and then to Brazil. From Brazil, I traveled by bus and on foot to Peru, Ecuador, Colombia, Panama, northward through all of Central America, and Mexico to reach the US. The entire trip cost US$18,000.

I left Bangladesh for political reasons. In 2015, I joined the Liberal Democratic Party (LDP). My country has had one-party rule for sixteen years, with the Awami League controlling the military and police. Only party members can vote. As a member of the opposition party, the LDP, I made political speeches, marched in protest, passed out leaflets, and joined sit-ins. The police monitored my political activity, and I knew my life was in danger. Only the threat of leaving my beautiful children fatherless and my wife a widow forced me to leave Bangladesh.

Do I have hope for significant change in my country? Not immediately. The LDP will have to grow bigger and stronger. Its membership has been growing in past years, but its growth has to accelerate more rapidly. In the meantime, I want to become a US citizen and bring my wonderful family to be with me in the US.

■　■　■

Police Knifed Me Four Times
in the Back

Being a twenty-seven-year-old Muslim with very little English poses many problems for me. My name is Mohammed Isujon. My home country is Bangladesh. I have little education, having spent only one month in a madrasa reciting the Holy Koran. I have come to the US because of my political problems caused by opposition to the government. The national police beat me up several times and then knifed me in the back in four different places. Here, Mr. Pace, let me show you my scars.

On February 28, 2019, I flew out of Bangladesh to India, Ethiopia, Brazil, and, finally, Peru. There I took a bus through Ecuador, Colombia, and Panama, and then continued on through all of Central America and Mexico to Matamoros, Mexico. The total cost of the trip was US$20,000. It was a long trip. It took me five months to reach Matamoros. I stayed in the tent city near the bridge for twenty days, and then I swam across the Rio Grande to the US. Before that, in Matamoros, the police handed me over to a drug cartel who blindfolded me, beat me up, and forced me to squat for hours at a time. They also extorted me for US$4,000.

US immigration authorities held me for eight days, and released me today, December 4th. I will be going by bus tonight to New York City to stay with a family friend. It is such a relief to be freed from the fear of more torture.

■　■　■

Policeman Killed by Another Policeman

My name is Ms. Mayin Hernández, twenty years old, from Chalatenango, El Salvador. I took one semester studying nutrition at the university. I have twin brothers, three years old, and an older sister, thirty-two years old. My father was a police lieutenant.

While in high school, I participated in a student protest with eight others, and the police beat us up. I went to the police station to protest; they beat me again. When I cried out that what they were doing was against the law, the policemen just laughed at me. During that period, my father's partner was killed by another policeman. When *papi* (father) appealed to higher authorities, they responded with: "Are you a guerilla?"

On June 28, 2019, I left Chalatenango with my dad's friend who helped pay for the trip. We had to walk part of the way, arriving in Reynosa, Mexico, on July 12th. The next day, I swam across the Rio Grande, close to the bridge. The *migra* (border patrol) took me to their headquarters in McAllen, Texas, where I stayed until transferred on July 15th to El Valle Detention Facility in Raymondville, Texas. I stayed at El Valle for eight months. Our treatment wasn't super, but okay. On February 4, 2020, I was released from El Valle, taken to the Brownsville bus station, and on to Good Neighbor Settlement House. This evening I will board a Greyhound bus to New York City where I will live with my female cousin. I'll take whatever job I can find. I am so happy to be here in the US!

■　■　■

Unique Experience in Chiapas

I come from a town of eighty thousand inhabitants: San Juan Chamula, Chiapas, Mexico. My name is Salvador Villarreal, twenty-eight years old, with twelve years of education. My wife's name is Erica Villagómez, twenty-five years old, with six years of education. Then there's baby Adolfo, only five-months old. I was a farmer producing corn and beans on two acres of rented land.

There was a lot of violence in San Juan Chamula, instigated mainly by the mayor. People were extorted for money, with bad consequences if they didn't pay up. However, I was neither extorted nor threatened; it was quite an experience! I was the only person I knew who was treated like that, but I felt I would not be spared forever. Therefore, I decided to leave my hometown.

My family and I boarded a bus on December 15th to come to the US, and reached Matamoros, Mexico, on the 17th. We lodged in the tent city, near the bridge to Brownsville, Texas. We received outstanding care from the volunteers of *Team Brownsville* while in the tent city. We crossed the border on December 23rd and spent one day in the US Border Patrol's headquarters, without being put in the *hielera* (cold storage detention room). Unheard of! Early on the morning of the 24th, we were transferred to the Brownsville bus station, and then on to the Good Neighbor Settlement House. We leave on the 6:30 p.m. Greyhound bus for Tampa, Florida. We'll live with my cousin, and I'll take whatever job I can find.

THE CALVARY
by Andrea Mantegna (1431–1506)
15th century. 0,76 x0,96 m. Louvre Museum, Paris (Photo by Josse/Leemage/
Contributor. Corbis Historical Collection via Getty Images).

AUTHOR'S NOTE: As with His unjust and barbarous crucifixion, Christ's death was the result of the High Priests of Judaea and their judicial body, the Sanhedrin, in concert with the governor of Roman Judaea, Pontius Pilate, rallying the crowds to demand that Jesus be crucified, not Barrabas, the murderer and insurrectionist, for allegedly challenging Roman law as "King of the Jews," a title given him by the people. Nevertheless, Roman law declared this statement a political crime whose penalty was crucifixion.

Gangs operating in modern civilization are protected by corrupt authoritarian governments and rulers to suppress challenges to their authority, hegemony, and territorial rights. Their innocent victims—rich, poor, truth-telling advocates, landowners, small farmers, students, people of faith—often meet a cruel death, victims of the lawlessness.

■　■　■

Chapter 3

GANGS

"Keep me as the apple of your eye;
  hide me in the shadow of your wings
  from the wicked who are out to destroy me,
  from my mortal enemies who surround me.

They close up their callous hearts,
and their mouths speak with arrogance.

They have tracked me down,
they now surround me, with eyes alert,
to throw me to the ground.
They are like a lion hungry for prey,
like a fierce lion crouching in cover.
Rise up, LORD, confront them, bring them down;
with your sword rescue me from the wicked."

PSALM 17:8–13
New International Version (NIV) Bible

Lucky to Be Alive

A twenty-eight-year-old Honduran with a degree from the National University of Honduras as an agroindustrial engineer, specializing in food refrigeration, I am one of the privileged ones with a great education. My name is José Eli Anariba, married with an eleven-month-old daughter named Elise Sebastián.

I owned my own business with three employees; it was very successful. My success was built on competence and service, developing a reputation with my clients and the community that I was very dependable.

Living in Comayagua, a city of one hundred fifty thousand, I, through my business success, attracted the attention of a *pandilla* (gang). They tried to extort me for $5,000 Lempiras (US$200). From other victims' experiences, I knew that if I paid the original $5,000 Lempiras, the next demand would be doubled to $10,000 Lempiras, and after that, how much more? If I didn't pay, they would kill me. I refused to pay, gave my car away at an extremely low price, kissed my wife and daughter goodbye, leaving them with my mother-in-law. I left Comayagua on June 30th by bus.

While traveling through the state of Veracruz, Mexico, the van we were in had a bad accident on July 6, 2019.[22] I suffered a bad concussion, a head wound requiring many stitches still with me today, and some broken ribs. I don't remember anything about the accident details, where it happened in Veracruz, or the hospital where I entered and remained

---

22 Méndez, Roberto. "Muere mujer indocumentada tras volcar automóvil en Alvarado." *eldictamen.mx,* 6 July, 2019, https://www.eldictamen.mx/veracruz/hechos /muere-mujer-indocumentada-tras-volcar-automovil-en-alvarado/.

for ten days. I lost everything . . . my clothes, my watch, cell phone, papers and passport, and all my money. The hospital's social services gave me the money and clothes to continue my journey to Reynosa, Mexico, where I crossed the Rio Grande and was taken to a hospital in McAllen, Texas, where I remained for eleven days. I spent one day in the Hidalgo, Texas, detention center and from there to the Brownsville bus station, and then to the Good Neighbor Settlement House.

I'm going to Fort Worth, Texas, to live with my father. There I hope to use my degree and experience to get a job within something in the food or refrigeration industry. At this point in my life, I give thanks to God, for I'm lucky to be alive!

■   ■   ■

Economía y Pandillas

(The Economy and Gangs)

My name is Emilia Calel Itsep, a Guatemalan forty-three-year-old mother of four: Medellín, age sixteen, Frank, age fourteen, Emma, age nine, and Berna, age six. Medellín has finished eleven years of school, and received his high school diploma. Our youngest, Berna, has finished the first grade of primary school. My husband, Julio Reales, age fifty, has been in New Jersey for three years where he works the night shift in a wholesale fish house.

Husband Julio had a good job as a chauffeur in Guatemala, but his income wasn't enough to sustain our large family, and, as a result, he was always in debt. In addition to his debt load, he was always being pressured by the *pandillas* (gangs) to pay them every week part of his earnings as a chauffeur. So he came to the US three years ago.

On June 15, 2019, my children and I left Guatemala, following my husband to the US. By truck and on foot, we reached Reynosa, Mexico, on July 15th, without having to pay a *coyote* (smuggler). People helped us along the way without charging a penny. We crossed the Rio Grande in a launch, walking for some two hours until we reached a big highway, and were picked up by the *migra* (border patrol) who took us to join other immigrants under a bridge, where we spent the rest of the night. My goodness! It was so cold under the bridge.

Then we were taken to the *migra's* headquarters where we spent two days in the *hielera* (cold storage detention room); it was very crowded and cold. From there, we spent several days in the detention center in

53

Hidalgo, Texas, where the food was surprisingly good. Now we are here in the Good Neighbor Settlement House preparing for our trip to New Jersey to join my husband. All my children will be in school by September, and I will be looking for a job. We will have a good life!

■　■　■

Man of All Seasons
Álvaro José Obando Martínez

Construction Engineer, Student Defender, Evangelical Pastor

JAMES PACE:

Álvaro Obando is a fifty-year-old Nicaraguan citizen who has been traveling to and fro, between the US and Nicaragua since 2006, mainly for business purposes. Having established himself in construction projects in Nicaragua, he then branched out to the US, concentrating in Kentucky and Tennessee. In 2012, Obando Construction was working mainly in Nashville, Tennessee, employing over one hundred W-2 employees for more than a year at the Music City Center and the Omni Nashville Hotel.

In a letter to a prospective client, Álvaro Obando states his company has expertise in metal and wood framing, drywall hanging, waterproofing, acoustic and hard ceilings and finishing . . . assisting you with completing your project in a timely efficient manner. [They] have enjoyed working on both small and large projects at all stages of a project . . . enjoying projects ranging in revenue from US$100,000 to US$4,000,000.

Successful businessman Obando is back in Managua, Nicaragua, in the spring of 2018 when university student protests break out over the government's mistreatment of its elderly citizens marching against the government's reduction of their social benefits. More than three hundred students are shot as they protest, and Álvaro Obando is one who rises to help them, as much as he can. He entered the fray in April, helping the students with food, and transporting the injured to various hospitals in Managua. By the end of May, he had received several death threats, but he persisted in helping the protesters.

On June 4th, while Obando was filling his gas tank, a new, expensive white van pulled up beside him, and six armed men jumped out, one of whom put a six-millimeter pistol to Obando's head and said, 'We have reports you are supporting the university protesters; this week will not pass that you will die along with your wife. You are part of the university vandals; you are on our death list.' To which Obando responded, he knew his rights, and there were plenty of witnesses present who could testify on his behalf. The accusers then sped off in their van at full speed.

Obando had already changed his residence to another township. On June 5th, he went to his former home, found the front door broken down, his house ransacked, and a warning in large letters: 'Traitor, we have you controlled.'

With the protection of the International Human Rights Center in Managua, Álvaro Obando and his wife Massiell Judíth fled to the US, via a short stop in El Salvador at the US Embassy. Upon arrival to the US, they were placed in the Port Isabel Detention Center, and Álvaro appointed himself evangelical pastor of his flock of inmates in the detention center. Drawing upon his experience as member and pastor of a congregation in Nicaragua, pastor Álvaro held worship services, Bible studies, counseling all who asked, living the life of a faithful disciple 24/7. He was finally released from detention in mid-October, and decided to enter La Posada Providencia in San Benito, Texas, where he could get legal help for his wife to secure the papers she needed to remain with him in the US. When asked if he was confident he could get the needed help for his wife, pastor Álvaro smiled.

ÁLVARO OBANDO:
The Lord will provide.

■   ■   ■

El Machetero

(The Machete Wielder)

Luís M. Ramos is my name, a thirty-six-year-old Guatemalan whose wife and two daughters live in Washington, DC. I only had seven years of school, and worked in sales in a fruit-and-vegetable store in the capital, Guatemala City.

I was a victim of an extortion racket, and had to pay protection money. At the end of the month, a member of a *pandilla* (gang) would hit me up for $2,000 Guatemalan Quetzales [US$250]. For one whole year, I paid those $2,000 Quetzales; there was very little left over to support myself. I knew if I didn't pay the full amount due, I ran the risk of being killed. Finally, I said to myself, 'Enough is enough,' and I told my collector from the *pandilla*, 'I'm not going to pay you any more.'

Several members of the *pandilla* grabbed me after I checked out of work, threw me in a car, blindfolded me, and drove me to an abandoned house. It must have been in *el campo* (the countryside), for there were no sounds outside, except some clucking hens. I was tied and bound to a chair, my arm was placed across a table, and a man sat on my hand. Then with one strong quick blow, my arm was cut off below my shoulder, halfway down to my elbow. A paramedic applied a tourniquet and stopped the flow of blood. I was blindfolded again, placed in a car, and then dumped at the entrance to a hospital in Guatemala City. All this occurred on May 16, 2017.

When I left the hospital, I knew I had to flee Guatemala, for the *pandilla* could not allow a man to live who had refused them and survived, and was still walking around Guatemala. On February 2, 2019, carrying nothing with me, I reached the Rio Grande by bus, arriving in Reynosa [Mexico]. A friend paid my launch fare to cross the Rio Grande on February 14th. After a one-hour walk, the *migra* (border patrol) picked me up, stuck me in the *hielera* (cold storage detention room) for two days, then another two days in the *hielera* in the Port Isabel Detention Center, where I stayed for a total of twenty-four days. The treatment at the detention center was good. Now I'm here at the Brownsville, Texas, bus station talking to you, Señor Pace, eager to get to Houston, Texas. I'm going to go job hunting as soon as possible. I've heard the grocery store chains like Fiesta, Kroger, and HEB may hire workers with my experience. They'll put in a good word for me, and help me snag (*pega*) a job.

■　　■　　■

Join or Else

We are a married couple coming to the US from El Salvador who have no children. I am Melvin Medlar Trejo, twenty-two years old, and my wife is Catarín Escobar de Trejo, twenty-four years old. We both received our twelfth-year diplomas which are equivalent to the first year of college in the US. Our hometown, Santa Ana, with three hundred thousand inhabitants, is in a mountainous region of El Salvador.

After finishing my formal education, I began work as a brick mason's helper; my wife, a homemaker. Members of a local *pandilla* (gang) approached me and threatened me either to join them or else . . . meaning getting beat up, possibly tortured, and, ultimately, death. There were approximately thirty-five *pandilla* members, including adults, youth, and several women. I was threatened once in December, 2018, and then again on January 19, 2019. I knew there would be no third time for just threats. A neighbor suggested I seek protection from the police, but I knew that was useless, for all of us with street-smarts viewed the police as being on the *pandilla's* payroll.

Within a day of the second threat, January 19th, my wife and I were on the bus to Guatemala. We passed through Guatemala in one day, but then obtaining a visa of safe conduct required a twenty-day wait near the border, in Tapachula [Chiapas]. Once in Monterrey, we waited from February 18th until July 1st, reaching Matamoros the next day. We sought refuge in the evangelical church, *El Buen Samaritano* (The Good Samaritan), and once our name came to the top of the list of asylum seekers waiting to enter America, we crossed the bridge to

Brownsville, Texas, on August 29th, and were taken to the Port Isabel Detention Center by the *migra* (US Border Patrol) that same day.

We were kept in the detention center for two months. We were released on October 28, 2019, and passed through the Brownsville, Texas, bus station on the way to the Good Neighbor Settlement House. We leave early on the 29th [of October] by bus to Atlanta, Georgia, where we'll live with my brother. I'll look for a job in construction upon arrival, for my wife is four months pregnant. Imagine the bills I'll have to pay for the birth of my child and the following months!

■   ■   ■

Too Much Violence
for a Family of Six

We are a large family from San Cristóbal de las Casas, Chiapas, Mexico. My name is Miguel Gómez Martín, forty-five years old, with only four years of education. My wife is Pascuala Pérez, thirty-eight years old, with no schooling. Then there's Josefina, seventeen, with six years of education; Moronita, fifteen, also six years of education; Luís Miguel, thirteen, and again six years of education; and, finally, Teresa, eight, with three years of primary school. I am a farmer, and grow corn on 1.1 acres of family land. Our family eats all the corn I can produce.

There is violence all around us in San Cristóbal caused by the *pandillas* (gangs). Rival *pandillas* have shoot-outs among themselves, and also kill citizens who refuse to join and work for them. I was one of those threatened with death, if I didn't join a *pandilla*. That was the straw that broke the camel's back . . . just too much violence threatening our family of six.

On February 1, 2020, we left San Cristóbal by bus, paying a *coyote* (smuggler) only $400 Mexican Pesos, approximately US$20 for his help. On February 4th, we arrived in Matamoros, Mexico. We stayed one day in the tent city close to the bridge to Brownsville, Texas; then on the 6th, we crossed the bridge and were detained for one day in the headquarters of the US Immigration Service. Now on February 7th, we're here at Good Neighbor Settlement House in Brownsville, waiting to take the 6:00 p.m. Greyhound bus to Tampa, Florida, where we'll live with my *cuñado* (brother-in-law). Once I get my papers from the federal judge, I'll take any job I can find.

■   ■   ■

Aviones de Esperanza

(Planes of Hope)

My name is Siantiacruz Méndez, a fifty-seven-year-old farmer from Cuajinicuilapa, Guerrero, Mexico. Accompanying me are my wife, Clementina Pérez, fifty-five years old, and my son, Samuel, six years old. I have only had three years of primary school, and my wife has had five. I farmed a small plot of family land for corn, beans, and chiles.

We had a lot of violence in Cuajinicuilapa. The *pandillas* (gangs) extorted money, threatened, and killed many people. We lived in constant fear. On October 12, 2019, we flew out of Guerrero to Los Cabos, Baja California, Mexico, and from there on our *avión de esperanza* (plane of hope) to Monterrey. We then took the bus to Matamoros, Mexico. There we stayed in a migrant house for two months, and crossed the Rio Grande by bridge to Brownsville, Texas, on December 2nd. We were placed in the *hielera* (cold storage detention room) by the *migra* (US Border Patrol) with ten other immigrants. We were given only a cold, old baloney sandwich, with a cup of juice.

Early on December 3rd, we were sent to the Brownsville bus station, and then on to the Good Neighbor Settlement House. Later tonight, we will board the bus to North Carolina. We'll be living with my twenty-four-year-old son who has a construction job. I hope to join him in construction, while wife Clementina will be the homemaker, since my son is a bachelor.

I am an Evangelical Pentecostal, and I give daily thanks to God, for He is watching over us on our planes of hope and our bus trip.

■   ■   ■

Against the Narcos

Lázaro is my nickname, for I have returned from near-death several times. A thirty-two-year-old Guatemalan, I had prepared to be a school teacher, but my wife, daughter, and I could not live on the meager salary of a Guatemalan school teacher. So I joined the National Civil Police, working with them for seven years, the last three of which I was assigned to the special unit of the *Comando Nacional Antiextorsión y Secuestro* (National Antikidnapping and Bribery Forces Command). Kidnapping and drug-running were interrelated, and as a captain in my unit, I lived under the constant pressure of being bought out by the drug smugglers.

I helped capture the number one drug trafficker in Guatemala, *El Negro Sosa* [a.k.a. Efraín Cifuentes González], the leader of the drug ring operating on the Guatemala–Mexico border. [Guatemala "is used for its geographic position as a bridge by the international cartels to move drugs from South America to the United States, passing through Mexico (*El país centroamericano es utilizado por su posición geográfica como puente por los carteles internacionales que trafican droga de Sudamérica hacia Estados Unidos, pasando por territorio mexicano.*)"[23]]. [*El Negro Sosa* had ties to the Zetas and Knights Templar, according

---

23 EFEDATA/AGENCIA EFE. "Capturan en Guatemala supuesto líder internacional del narcotráfico." *efedata.com,* 7 Nov 2014, https://efs.efeservicios.com/texto /capturan-guatemala-supuesto-lider-internacional-narcotrafico/18007113020. Used with Permission, 12 Aug 2021.

to investigations,[24] but he was considered a kingpin in the Sinaloa cartel trafficking in Guatemala]. He operated on behalf of El Chapo [Joaquín Guzmán Loera], the Mexican drug king recently sentenced to life imprisonment here in the United States. The violent and destructive Zetas drug cartel from Mexico was also very active in Guatemala, against which my Command was often engaged. On various occasions, I used a wire and camera not only on drug suspects, but also against my own superiors to protect myself and prove they were on the take [accepting bribes]. I lived like this for over a year, but then my superiors grew suspicious.

I was given an order which I knew was a setup to get me killed. So I refused to carry out the order, and was, therefore, put in detention for three days. I knew I was doomed. With the help of several friends, I escaped. For a year, I was living the life of a fugitive in Guatemala, and then I fled to the United States, arriving on November 16, 2018. Twice the gangs tried to kidnap me, once in Reynosa and then at the edge of the Rio Grande. I escaped both attempts; at the river, I dived in and swam across to get away from my captors.

I was in El Valle Detention Facility in Raymondville, Texas, for three-and-a-half months. I won't go into all the details of my treatment there, which I know others have done. The most important point I want to make is the authorities at El Valle play with your mind; they get in your head, by giving you contradictory orders. For instance, they give you two towels, then an official comes by and says, 'You're supposed to have only one towel; go back and turn in one of the towels.' So you turn it in. Then another official appears and says, 'You're supposed to have two towels; go get another towel.' When that charade is done to you three or four times, you don't know which end is up, and begin to question your own sanity. But, I met

---

24 Sánchez, Glenda. "Prensa Libre, Negro Sosa va a debate por narcotráfico." *prensalibre.com,* 17 Sept. 2016, https://www.prensalibre.com/guatemala/justicia /negro-sosa-va-a-debate-por-narcotrafico/.

and accepted Jesus Christ as my Lord and Savior two months ago in El Valle Detention Facility; He has given me the strength to live a life of peace, even in the midst of the upset of living in El Valle. I trust that this quality of life will continue for me in the years ahead here in the US.

■   ■   ■

The Shoemaker

My name is Michael Quintero, a twenty-one-year-old shoemaker from San Salvador, El Salvador. Javier is my three-year-old son who keeps me constantly moving, as I take care of him. I specialize in creating women's sandals, and my nineteen-year-old sister took care of the business part, including the heavy tax load present in today's El Salvador.

Then one night, I was robbed of all my hand tools and some personal items. I knew I would be in trouble if I denounced the robbers, probably killed, but I went ahead and did it. I got my tools and personal belongings back, and immediately sold the tools. Then with the money from the sale, and additional financial help from an uncle, I fled the country with son, Javier. All this happened in less than three weeks . . . all so fast.

I often can't believe it. You know, what happened to me is happening all over El Salvador.

Now to look to my future. Javier and I will start a new life in North Carolina with my uncle and his two sons. They've invited me to join them in the moving van company where they work. So it's on to North Carolina!

■　■　■

Thankful to Be Alive

Inmer Hitay is my name, a thirty-seven-year-old Guatemalan farmer with no formal schooling. My beloved mother had fourteen children; my spouse, Blanca Isabel, has three children. Thank God we five are here together and safe in the US.

On September 18, 2018, at 2:00 a.m., our home was robbed by a gang of ten men armed with shotguns. We recognized them, and in the following weeks we told our neighbors what had happened and the robbers' identities. We never thought about the consequences of our speaking out.

On November 20th at 3:00 a.m., the same gang returned and tried to kill us by blasting four salvos from their shotguns at close range, damaging both the exterior and interior of our home, concentrating on Blanca Isabel's and my bedroom. I still have some shot left in my fingers, but Blanca Isabel took the full effect of several shots . . . in her right leg, right arm, but worst of all, her head. The doctor had to cut a straight line across the length of her head to remove all the buckshot, before stitching it up. I shudder every time I look at the photograph of Blanca Isabel's head. I noticed your turning away from the photo when I showed it to you, Señor Pace. She came so close to death, but there she is now, sitting and laughing with our children, with a full head of hair. A blessing.

That same gang went on to kill five nearby neighbors, and ten more only five hundred meters distant. The authorities? As usual, they were bought. As the saying goes, their silence was deafening!

We left our home the same day, my wife staying in a hospital in a nearby town for seven days. Then we left by bus with a [safe conduct] visa issued by Mexico, stopping in Tenosique, Tabasco, near Villahermosa, and helped by Mexican immigration authorities. We continued by bus to Matamoros. Total trip time: forty-five days. There we waited for a month, before crossing to the US. In passing, I want to thank brother Mike Benavides and his volunteers for their help while at the bridge . . . hot food, blankets, tarps, clothes, etc. I got tired of waiting, so with my sons I constructed a crude wooden raft, and then in my boxer shorts, swam and pushed the raft with my family aboard. The *migra* (border patrol) was awaiting us on the other side, underneath the bridge.

We were taken to the Port Isabel Detention Center on March 1st, and released today, March 4, 2019, because our case was considered a special case. Today, we are going to Houston to live with a friend for a time. There, nineteen-year-old son Juveni will complete his final university year, with a BS in computer sciences. Daughter Perla, sixteen, is in her third year of high school, and Mailawe, eight, in her second year of primary. My wife, Blanca Isabel, and I will be smiling and praising the Lord for giving us *la yapa de la vida* (the bonus days of life)!

■　■　■

As Soon As Possible

Pablo Ramírez is my pseudonym. I'm a twenty-six-year-old Honduran with a twenty-four-year-old wife, and a two-year-old daughter. I was the sole owner of my business, selling the favorite fruits and vegetables of my fellow Hondurans. I built up a good business; my produce was always fresh. I sprinkled my leafy vegetables every three to four hours daily, to keep them sparkling. The town's housewives were my best advertisers, spreading the word, 'If you want fresh vegetables at good prices, buy from young Pablito.'

Then I fell under the forced protection of one of the local *pandillas* (gangs), like what I've heard you Americans have experienced with the protection of the mafia in big cities. They pressured me for some time to accept their protection; I kept stalling, but I knew my stalling couldn't continue much longer. Finally, I agreed to start paying 12 to 15 percent of my monthly net income for their protection. Otherwise, they would kill me. For nearly three years, I paid, and along with the heavy taxes I paid to the local, state, and federal government, I didn't have much left for my family. The police were of no help; they were on the gang's payroll. I even had to tip the local policeman who serviced my market every Saturday, my best business day.

After much planning, and leaving my wife and daughter in the care of my parents, one Saturday night after kissing the family goodbye, I just disappeared and headed for the United States. I felt bad about leaving the family, but my wife strongly urged me to go.

What am I going to do? I'm leaving the bus station here in Brownsville, Texas, in a couple of hours to go to Houston to live with my sister and brother-in-law. He works in construction, and she takes care of dogs. You ask me when are my wife and little girl coming to Houston? That's easy . . . just as soon as possible.

■　■　■

A Man of Faith Standing Firm

My name is Bryan Santiago Toatpanta, twenty years old, from Quito, Ecuador. My family consists of my father, five brothers and sisters. For ten years, I worked in a store selling fruit and vegetables. Recently, in the fall of 2018, the *narcotraficantes* (drug traffickers) started to pressure me to join them and sell drugs. I told them, 'No,' several times, and each time they beat me up. One day they said, 'If you continue to say no, we'll kill you.'

I am an evangelical Roman Catholic. I attend mass faithfully; I read and study the Bible; I pray to God to know His will for my life. There's no way I can join a drug gang to poison the youth of my country. I am a Christian!

My father agreed with my decision to come to the US. He helped me, and paid for most of the trip. On December 18th, I left Ecuador. I hired a *coyote* (smuggler) to get me through Mexico, but by paying him in installments, little by little, I only paid him half of the US$6,000 for which I had contracted him. I crossed into the US in Brownsville, Texas, on January 1st, and from there, [I spent] two months in the Port Isabel Detention Center. I learned a lot from my neighbors in the detention center, and am very grateful to them . . . a hearty thanks to them and my Lord God.

■ ■ ■

Even Domestic Help Threatened

Being a forty-four-year-old Guatemalan domestic worker, I have great family responsibility, with children ages fifteen, thirteen, and three. My name is Elvira Maldonado, living in the municipality of San Ildefonso Ixtahuacán, Huehuetenango, Guatemala, with some forty-four thousand inhabitants.

Even though domestic work pays very little, it's very ironic that a local *pandilla* (gang) demanded a cut of my pay. I refused to pay. So the *pandilla* took my two oldest children. With the financial help of my larger family, I left Guatemala on March 12, 2019, in an eighteen-wheel trailer, which cost $20,000 Quetzales, approximately US$2,500.

On March 24th, I crossed the Rio Grande in a launch, spent two days in the *hielera* (cold storage detention room), and one day in the Port Isabel Detention Center. Now I'm here at the Good Neighbor Settlement House in Brownsville, Texas, on March 28th, eager to get to Maryland to live with my sister-in-law of seven years.

■　■　■

My Spanish Is Not Very Good

JAMES PACE:

The man I wanted to interview was talking on his cell phone which was plugged into a floor-level outlet, requiring him to kneel on the floor. His wife faced me, seated at the end of the table, with a sleeping baby wrapped in a cloth sling on her back. There was a three- to four-year-old child stretched on the floor behind her *papi* (father) playing with a floor-length window curtain, glancing up to me occasionally. This scene continued for more than five minutes, until *papi* had finished his conversation in an indigenous language he later identified as Tzotzil [a Mayan language spoken by the indigenous Tzotzil Maya people in the Mexican state of Chiapas]. Meet the Alberto Gómez Gómez family from a village near Chiapas, Mexico, near the Guatemalan border. Husband, Alberto Gómez, twenty-five years old; wife, Veronica, twenty-three years old, daughters Rosanna, four years old, and Alicia, one year old.

As soon as I told Alberto I wanted to interview him, he immediately responded he didn't understand Spanish very well. I reassured him my questions would be simple and easy to understand. So I deliberately spoke slowly, a little louder than usual, using simple words and sentences. Between my question and his response, there was always a short pause, during which I knew he was processing Spanish to Tzotzil, and then back to Spanish, to answer me. We did quite well. Wife Veronica had been very unresponsive when I first sat down. She wouldn't answer nor acknowledge my greeting verbally or facially. By the end of the interview, she was standing up, smiling and looking directly at me; she only spoke her native language Tzotzil.

Alberto is a farmer renting the land where he grows beans and corn. His is strictly subsistence farming. He wanted to leave his village because of the violence. There was a group of men in the village who wanted to control life there; just two years ago, they killed the president of their village. The same group constantly pressured Alberto to join them; he was afraid if he didn't join, they would also kill him, and what would happen to his wife and daughters?

After securing the proper papers, they all left Chiapas by bus on August 5, 2019. By August 7th, they arrived in Matamoros, Mexico, and waited only half a day below the bridge, before crossing the Rio Grande. They were detained two days at the *migra* (border patrol) headquarters. Alberto spent the two days in the *hielera* (cold storage detention room), but Veronica and the children did not have to endure that inhumane treatment. Now on the 9th, they are here at the Good Neighbor Settlement House, leaving tonight for Tampa, Florida. Living with his older brother and family, Alberto will look for whatever work he can find.

■   ■   ■

Between a Rock and a Hard Place

I am Gregorio Heredia Gómez, thirty-two years old, from a town of three thousand three hundred inhabitants, San Juan Chamula, in Chiapas, Mexico, along the Guatemalan border. Accompanying me are my wife, Juana Catarina Pérez Pérez, twenty-four years old, and my son, Cruz Damián, nine years old, and daughter, Julia Esmeralda, three years old. Both my wife and I finished primary school. I'm a farmer growing corn, beans, and green vegetables on 1.2 acres of land; our family consumed everything we grew.

In our town of San Juan Chamula, there were always two political groups—one group controlling town government, and the other group trying to kick them out and take over control of the township. Both groups played for keeps; every year at least one person was killed. Changing sides was no answer; those who had been friends were now enemies . . . one never could satisfy both sides. This constant conflict caused all the schools and the town clinic to be closed.

On August 27, 2019, we left our town by car. It was a long trip. We had very little money, so it took us five weeks to get to Matamoros. Once there, we stayed for a month in an immigrant refuge. On October 28th, we crossed the bridge to Brownsville, Texas. We passed one night in the *migra's* (US border patrol's) headquarters, and today we've gone through the Brownsville bus station, and on to the Good Neighbor Settlement House. At 10:00 p.m. tonight, we're on our way to Tampa, Florida, to live with my older brother. I'll take whatever job I can find.

■   ■   ■

Too Much Violence

I come from the city of Cuernavaca, state of Morelos, Mexico. Since the time of the Aztecs, Cuernavaca has served as a health center, vacation spot, and preferred living area for politicians, and the wealthy of Mexico City.

In contrast to the special groups of Cuernavaca, I am a simple gardener, Pedro Castro, twenty-eight years old, with wife Daram, twenty years old, and sons, Andrés, two years old, and Pedro, one year old. I only finished the six years of primary school, and Daram, eight years of middle school.

You ask why I brought my family to the US. Today Cuernavaca is a city of violence caused by the *pandillas* (gangs), and the authorities respond, in kind. Not a day goes by without shootings with all kinds of weapons and a few grenades thrown in for good measure. I do not want to live and try to raise my family with death threatening us daily, even for a simple gardener and kin. You even told me, Señor Pace, that your daughter and family had fled Cuernavaca a good number of years ago. Now it's our turn.

On November 14, 2019, we left Cuernavaca traveling by bus to Matamoros, Mexico, without any help from a *coyote* (smuggler). There we stayed in the tent city near the bridge to Brownsvillle, Texas, receiving wonderful help from the volunteers of *Team Brownsville* of two ample meals daily, blankets, clothes, and rain gear. After seven days in the tent city, we crossed the bridge to Brownsville, and passed through the bus station to the Good Neighbor Settlement House. So here we are in GNSH leaving today, November 22nd at 10:30 p.m. by bus for Ohio, where we will live with my aunt.

Now that we're here in the US, I'm beginning to wonder if we haven't traded the violence in Cuernavaca for the individual and mass shootings in this country. As the *dicho* (saying) goes, 'out of the frying pan and into the fire'!

■　■　■

Life Together

We are a family of four from Honduras: Marvin Núñez, thirty-two years old, Wendy Silva, thirty-one years old, twins José and Noel Núñez, eight years old. Both Marvin and Wendy finished twelve years of schooling, with Marvin's favorite subject science, and Wendy's, mathematics. We're a family that lives together, works together, and plays together. We have a wonderful life together!

Marvin and Wendy worked together in a hardware store for thirteen years, for a good employer who paid very adequate salaries. However, the last two years they were extorted by a *pandilla* (gang) for 25 percent of their gross salaries. We were told, 'If you don't pay us, we'll kill you.'

On August 1, 2019, we left town by bus, paying a *coyote* (smuggler) US$6,000 for the four of us. Part of the money went for bribing the police en route, for we had no papers. On August 20th, we arrived to Reynosa, Mexico, where we stayed in the *coyote's* stash house for four days. Then at four in the afternoon, we crossed the Rio Grande on a *balsa* (inflatable raft) carrying ten passengers.

The *migra* (US Border Patrol) grabbed us within five minutes, and took us to the *pollera* (cage) for a day, and then down to the tent city detention center in Donna, Texas, where we stayed for seven days, until we were deported back to Matamoros, Mexico, on August 29, 2019. There we stayed in the tent city near the new bridge to Brownsville, Texas, and crossed the Rio Grande over the bridge on November 8th.

Now we're here at the Good Neighbor Settlement House, and at 10:00 p.m., we are leaving by bus to San Francisco, California, to stay with an aunt who has an office-cleaning business. She needs more workers, and has already guaranteed us jobs. I'll take a job immediately, but Wendy will have to wait, for she's eight months pregnant.

■　　■　　■

The Same Old Story

We are a large family: Lorenzo Díaz Díaz, thirty-eight years old; Carolina Jiménez, thirty years old; Guillermo, seventeen years old; Lorenzo, fifteen years old; Dulce Angélica, seven years old; and Ezequiel, one year old. We are from Yolonhuitz, Chamula, Chiapas, a small town of five hundred inhabitants. I have had four years of schooling, and my wife, none. I am a farmer, growing beans and corn on five acres of rented land. Our family is greatly blessed by the Lord and our membership in the Evangelical Pentecostal Church.

There is great injustice in Yolonhuitz due to warring political groups. Every week there are one or more killings. It's the same old story in our home town, constant killings. I didn't want to subject my children to living in such a situation, so we boarded a bus out of Chiapas on October 18th, arriving in Matamoros, Mexico, on the 20th. There we stayed in the tent city near the bridge over the Rio Grande for fifty days. A wonderful group of volunteer angels, *Team Brownsville*, provided us two hot meals daily, blankets, rain gear, clothes, shoes, and educational activities for both children and adults.

Early on the morning of December 3rd, we crossed the bridge, passed through the Brownsville, Texas, bus station, and are now here in the Good Neighbor Settlement House. We will leave tonight by bus for South Carolina where we'll stay with my sister. I'll look for whatever job I can find.

■　■　■

The Quiet One

I come from a town of three thousand inhabitants, Llano Grande-Sierra Norte, Oaxaca, Mexico. My name is Moisés González, a twenty-three-year-old university graduate, with a major in computers. My wife, Jasmín Bernal, is a twenty-two-year-old university graduate with a major in reading. We have a one-year-old daughter, Evangelina.

We were threatened with death by a *pandilla* (gang); they had already killed my brother. They tried to beat me up, but I defended myself successfully. I went to the police, but, as usual, they took no action, for they were on the gang's payroll.

On October 29, 2019, we took a bus from Oaxaca, without the help of a smuggler. Arriving to Matamoros, Mexico, on November 5th, we immediately went to the tent city near the bridge to Brownsville, Texas. While at the tent city, we received the wonderful help from the volunteers of *Team Brownsville* twice daily. Upon crossing the bridge, we were detained by the *migra* (US Border Patrol) for two days and then released for processing at the Brownsville bus station, and on to the Good Neighbor Settlement House on December 5th. We will leave Brownsville today, December 6th, for Salt Lake City, [Utah] where we will live with the pastor of a Christian Evangelical Church. Hopefully, I will find a job in computers.

AUTHOR'S NOTE: This interview is titled *The Quiet One*, for my Christian brother spoke very softly, barely moving his lips, and scarcely opening them. This resulted in his leaning toward me, and my leaning toward him.

■　■　■

No More Tourism

My name is Pascuale Santis Gómez, a thirty-two-year-old carpenter from San Cristóbal de las Casas, Chiapas, Mexico. I'm accompanied by my wife, Elisi, thirty-two years old, and son, Elisi Jesús, ten years old. Our hometown, San Cristóbal de las Casas with one hundred eighty-six thousand inhabitants, has been a tourist attraction for many years. People from all over the world come to view our indigenous festival clothing, listen to our indigenous spoken language which sounds like the twittering of birds, enjoy our various food dishes, and buy our pottery and paintings. Tourism enriched our economy. However, when the *pandillas* (gangs) came on the scene, pushing their dope and killing local citizens, except for a few daring souls, the tourists went somewhere else.

When I refused to join a *pandilla* and sell marijuana and hard drugs, gang members beat me up, and threatened to kill me. That's when I decided I couldn't live in San Cristóbal any more. I boarded a bus on December 21, 2019, and after an uneventful two-day trip, I reached Matamoros, Mexico. My family and I then went to live in the tent city near the bridge crossing the Rio Grande to Brownsville, Texas. There we received the wonderful care of *Team Brownsville.*

Early on the morning of December 12th, we crossed the bridge, were processed through the Brownsville bus station, and then on to the Good Neighbor Settlement House. We'll take a bus to Tampa, Florida, at 6:00 p.m. to live with my wife's cousin. I'll take whatever available job, but hopefully in construction as a carpenter.

■   ■   ■

Chapter 4

FAMILY

"Then Jesus' mother and brothers arrived. Standing outside, they sent someone in to call him. A crowd was sitting around him, and they told him, 'Your mother and brothers are outside looking for you.' 'Who are my mother and my brothers?' he asked.

Then he looked at those seated in a circle around him and said, 'Here are my mother and my brothers!'"

MARK 3:31–34
New International Version (NIV) Bible

AP Photo/Julia Le Duc
THE BODIES OF SALVADORAN MIGRANT OSCAR ALBERTO MARTÍNEZ RAMÍREZ AND
HIS NEARLY 2-YEAR-OLD DAUGHTER VALERIA LIE ON THE BANK OF THE RIO GRANDE
IN MATAMOROS, MEXICO, ON JUNE 24, 2019, AFTER THEY DROWNED TRYING TO CROSS
THE RIVER TO BROWNSVILLE, TEXAS.

"Now their names rise off her tongue: Say *Óscar y Valeria*. He swam
from Matamoros across to Brownsville, the girl slung around his neck,
stood her in the weeds on the Texas side of the river, swore to return
with her mother in hand, turning his back as fathers do who later say:
I turned around and she was gone. In the time it takes for a bird to hop
from branch to branch, Valeria jumped in the river after her father.
Maybe he called out her name as he swept her up from the river;
maybe the river drowned out his voice as the water swept them away.
Tania called out the names of the saints, but the saints drowsed
in the stupor of birds in the dark, their cages covered with blankets.
The men on patrol would never hear their pleas for asylum, watching
for *floaters*, hearts pumping coffee all night on the Texas side of the river."

Excerpt from "Floaters" from *Floaters: Poems*
by Martín Espada
2021 National Book Awards Poetry Winner

When Family Reunited?

I am a forty-year-old Cuban female who longs to be reunited with my husband and two children. My pseudonym is Sandra Limón. My husband and I flew to [French] Guiana on June 26th, leaving our son and daughter behind in Cuba with friends. Then we passed through Brazil to Uruguay where we stayed for three months working to help finance the trip. Back we went through Brazil, over to Peru, and up through Ecuador, and into Colombia. The three days required to reach Panama were tough, for we had to walk through the very thick jungle growth of the *Selva de Darién* (Jungle of Darién) which includes having to climb the infamous *Loma de la Muerte* (Ridge of Death). We were exhausted upon arriving in Panama.

We believed we had passed through all our challenges, but in Nicaragua we were detained for being *gusanos* [literal translation is "worms," but in Cuba it means "any reactionary, counter-revolutionary person"] and *Traidores a la Revolución Cubana* (Traitors to the Cuban Revolution). Luckily, our detention was only for three days. We paid our fine, and hit the road northward once again, passing through Honduras and Guatemala without any more incidents. Upon reaching Mexico City, we flew to Matamoros, and crossed the bridge to Brownsville, Texas.

I spent seventy days in the Port Isabel Detention Center. Although called a detention center, it's run like a prison, and without many of the amenities of a real prison. My experience there was so difficult that I don't want to talk about it. I'll just say my days there were *fuerte* (tough). For some unknown reason, my husband was first transferred out of

87

Port Isabel to a detention center in Alabama, then to one in Maryland, and now my love is in Boston. I have not talked to him since he left Port Isabel. Presently, I can only go to my female cousin's in Miami and await word from my husband when he's released in Boston. *¡Qué vida!* (What a life!) When will my family ever be reunited? *¿Quién sabe?* (Who knows?)

But despite all my worries and troubles, I do want to thank you and the volunteers here for all of your help.

■　■　■

For Our Children

My name is Lorenzo Villa, forty-six years old, with only one year of education. We're from Zacatlán, Puebla, Mexico. I'm accompanied by my wife, Nanci Martínez, thirty-seven years old, with six years of education; Corende L., fifteen years old; Bales, thirteen years old; Marte, eleven years old; Jesús, nine years old; Eduardo, eight years old; and Nazaret, six years old. Quite a family! Our children are loving, smart, and obedient. I am a farmer, working six acres of rented land, growing corn, beans, tomatoes, papayas, chiles, squash, and jalapeños.

There is a lot of violence in our town caused by the *pandillas* (gangs). They have kidnapped twelve- and thirteen-year-old boys and girls from middle school, and raped them; forced both youth and adults to sell drugs with severe consequences, including death, if they refuse to cooperate. Anyone going to the open-air market is subject to being caught in the crossfire of two rival *pandillas*. Our family has not been subject to any of this violence up until now, except for our nerves, but we know that one day our time to suffer will come. As the father and protector of our family, I decided to safeguard our children, and bring them to the US.

On December 12, 2019, our family flew out of Zihuatanejo to Monterrey, Mexico. The next day, we took the bus to Matamoros. For fifteen days, we stayed in the tent city near the bridge to Brownsville, Texas, where the volunteers of *Team Brownsville* helped us in so many different ways; we called them *nuestros angelitos* (our little angels). Today, December 29th, we'll board a Greyhound Bus to Tulsa, Oklahoma, where we'll stay with a friend. I hope to get a job in agriculture.

■   ■   ■

Our Family

Keeping our family together is of the greatest importance to my husband and me. Therefore, when we decided we could no longer live in Honduras and would come to the US, we all were coming to the US! Husband: Héctor Alejandro Bengthson, forty-eight years old; sons Johan Alejandro Bengthson, five years old, and Adara Alejandro Bengthson, ten years old; and wife, Belkin Yohana Espinosa de Bengthson, thirty-six years old.

We lived in the city of La Ceiba, Honduras with some two hundred four thousand inhabitants. My husband was a farmer with fifteen *manzanas* (thirty-seven acres) of orange trees. I was a school teacher for nineteen years, fifteen in primary and the last four years in kindergarten. I loved teaching the children in kindergarten. Life in Honduras is very expensive, with exorbitant prices for most items. In addition, the government is very corrupt and the *pandillas* (gangs) are running wild, and stronger than the police.

We left La Ceiba on June 8, 2019, traveling by auto to San Pedro Sula, Honduras. Taking a bus through Guatemala and Mexico, we reached Reynosa, Mexico, on June 16th, by paying a *coyote* (smuggler) US$11,000 to cross the Rio Grande in a launch. The *migra* (border patrol) detained us approximately one kilometer downstream from one of the Reynosa bridges. At the *migra* headquarters, we were placed in the *hielera* (cold storage detention room) for two days, and then on to the Hidalgo, Texas, detention center where we were confined in the *hielera* upon arrival and departure. Has anyone determined why the American authorities use the *hielera* so much?

Then we were taken to the Brownsville, Texas, bus station, and from there to here at the Good Neighbor Settlement House. We're now preparing for our trip to Nashville, Tennessee, where we'll be staying with the wife of my husband's nephew. My husband will take whatever job he can find, and once I can master some English and get my teacher's certificates recognized, I will resume teaching. Our family will still be united!

■   ■   ■

A Quick Trip

This has been a very quick trip! We left Chiapas, Mexico, near the Guatemalan border on Friday, August 2nd, and here we are at the Good Neighbor Settlement House, Brownsville, Texas, Monday, August 5th. I wonder why?*

My name is Héctor Díaz García, thirty-one years old, with wife Lucía López, twenty-nine years old; daughter, Deysi, eleven years old; and son, Óscar, four years old. A farmer growing onions and corn, our family only has a little more than an acre to farm with intermittent rain. Wife Lucía is a mother and housewife. We felt unfortunate because we didn't have our own house for various reasons.

As already mentioned, we left Guatemala on August 2, 2019, making a direct trip by bus without any difficulties. Reaching Matamoros, Mexico, on the 4th at 1:00 p.m., we took a taxi to the bridge and walked across it. On the US side, the *migra* (border patrol) detained us for one day, putting us in the *hielera* (cold storage detention room), which was very cold and crowded. From there, we were taken to the Good Neighbor Settlement House, and tomorrow we are going by bus to North Carolina to live with my brother-in-law who works as a gardener. Once there, Óscar will be in kindergarten, Deysi in fifth grade, and I will be looking for a job in gardening or farming.

■ ■ ■

AUTHOR'S NOTE:

The family's quick trip was due to the US administration's recent policy of allowing asylum seekers to enter rapidly, if they did not pass through a country where they had not refused available asylum—in their case, Mexico.

Hope for My Children

My name is Carina Morales, a twenty-four-year-old mother from Cuajinicuilapa, Guerrero, Mexico. I finished my twelfth year of secondary education, with my favorite subject being Spanish. I do not speak an indigenous language. My three children are Krizzaly Prudente, eight years old; Alexis, five years old; and Erick, eight months old. In Cuajinicuilapa, I worked in a small restaurant, mainly featuring tacos, coffee and soft drinks. It had a large family table inside and a healthy take-out taco business.

I fled my hometown because of a problem my younger brother had with a local *pandilla* (gang). He fled, and has not returned. If he does return, gang members have said they will not only kill him, but will make our mother and other family members suffer the consequences of his actions. You ask, Señor Jaime, 'Why didn't you go to the police?' You know the answer, if you know Mexico. The police are useless; they're on the *pandilla's* payroll!

So now we're here in Brownsville, Texas, having had an uneventful trip from Cuajinicuilapa to Matamoros, Mexico. We're going to live in Utah with my older brother and his family; he is in the home construction business. I will take whatever job I can find. In response to your question, Señor Jaime, of my dreams for my children, they are the same as any parent's: namely, that they finish school, get well-paying jobs, have families, be happy, and are good Christians and loyal US citizens. That's the hope and dream for my family.

■ ■ ■

Nothing Spectacular

CRISTINA JIMÉNEZ:
I don't know why you want to interview me, Señor Pace. My life has been very common, and nothing interesting happened on our trip to the US. So why me?

JAMES PACE:
Thus began my interview with Cristina Jiménez of Chiapas, Mexico, near the Guatemalan border. "Don't you worry, for I want my readers to know that many of the asylum seekers coming to the US are just regular people, or, as we say in Texas, just plain folks. Besides, I want to spend some time describing your four-year-old daughter Marisol; she's a cutie."

Daughter Marisol is a beautiful child with sparkling, black eyes and hair tied in a pony tail. She's very active, can't sit still, all over her mother while standing on a chair behind *mami* (mother) with arms around her, seeking *mami's* attention. Then she starts combing her mom's hair, braiding and unbraiding it, until Marisol is satisfied with the results. With an impish smile, she gets off the chair, ducks under the table where they are sitting, and begins to play peek-a-boo with me, seated a short distance away.

Twenty-eight year old Cristina, mother and homemaker, has had a rough life in Chiapas. In her words, her husband had abandoned them. In order for Cristina to support herself and Marisol, with an eye to her daughter's future, she planned to start a new life in her cousin's home with his family in Orlando, Florida. On July 29, 2019, they boarded a bus in Chiapas, and two days later they were in Matamoros, Mexico, across the river from Brownsville, Texas. They waited one day underneath the old railroad bridge; then they walked across the bridge, where they were detained by the *migra* (border patrol), and immediately taken to the Brownsville bus station. From there they were taken to the Good Neighbor Settlement House, where this interview occurred. That same evening, mother and daughter boarded a Greyhound bus for Orlando. Cristina will be looking for a job, and Marisol will attend kindergarten.

■   ■   ■

I Have to Hurry

My name is Wendy Romero Tejada, a twenty-one-year-old Honduran mother with four-year-old son, Edgar. I only finished the third grade of primary school, and, eventually, became a homemaker, living in great poverty. On leaving my son with his grandparents, I boarded a bus in Honduras on August 3, 2019, and headed to the US. It was an uneventful trip.

After arriving in Reynosa, I had to stay there three to four weeks, until I could cross the bridge over the Rio Grande. The *migra* (US Border Patrol) took me to their headquarters in McAllen, Texas, where I stayed for fourteen days, nine of them in the *hielera* (cold storage detention room). Imagine my being in that inhumane *hielera* for so long when I am seven months pregnant. I then was returned to Reynosa, where I stayed in a migrant shelter for forty-five days, and, once again, back to the US, where I stayed in a house for another fifteen days.

Now I'm here at the Good Neighbor Settlement House in Brownsville, Texas, and will leave today, November 4th, at 6:30 p.m. to go to Florida to live with a friend. I've got to hurry; I'm keeping my fingers crossed because I am nine months pregnant. Can you imagine having to give birth en route to Florida? Oh, Lord, help me.

■ ■ ■

A Mother's Boy

I am a twenty-three-year-old Guatemalan young man living in the valley of southeastern Guatemala, in the town of Chiquimula. My name is Elmer Jeovani Feastume. I live with my mama and two brothers. I have a primary school education, and have never worked outside my home. People may think it's strange a twenty-three-year-old man has never worked, but that's the way mama wants it.

Three times a local *pandilla* (gang) wanted me to join them, and they told me if I don't join the *pandilla*, they'll kill me. To try to persuade me the last two times, they beat me up, knocking the wind out of me. Why, I've never even doubled up my fists, much less fought anyone! My friends have always called me a sissy, my mama's pet.

On July 8, 2019, I left Guatemala with a group. Each one of us had to pay US$5,000 to a *coyote* (smuggler) to put us on the US side of the Rio Grande. On August 8th, we arrived to Reynosa. At dawn we crossed the river on a *balsa* (rubber pontoon). We walked to an open gate of the famous wall, and, on the other side, the *migra* (US Border Patrol) picked us up. They took us to their headquarters, where we stayed for three days. Then we were transferred to the *pollera* (immigrant holding pen) in Donna, Texas, for two days. Finally, they moved us to the Port Isabel Detention Center on August 7, 2019, where we stayed until August 22nd. They treated us well, but the food left a lot to be desired. My money for the trip was late to arrive, so I stayed at the Good Neighbor Settlement House. Now I am leaving by bus on August 29th at 10:00 p.m. for Atlanta, Georgia, to live with my uncle. It's going to feel funny looking for a job!

■   ■   ■

When Will We Be Together?

I am waiting . . . waiting to be with my husband again. You see, I went before the federal immigration judge as an asylum seeker on October 15th, and was given provisional asylum. On the same day, my husband went before a federal judge, and since he had no papers (I had them all), he was denied entry, and rescheduled for a hearing on December 12, 2019. From the Good Neighbor Settlement House, I will go on to Pennsylvania to wait for my husband.

My name is Dayana Rojas Pérez, a twenty-five-year-old Cuban. My husband of ten years, José Antonio Rodríguez, is twenty-six years old. We have fraternal twins who are one year old, still in Cuba. We lived in Guantánamo, and life in our town was completely separate from the US prison of Guantánamo. I finished *secundaria* (high school), and then went to the University of Medical Sciences, specializing as a dentist. Husband José Antonio finished high school, but had just one year as a preuniversity student because he had to give three years of military service.

All of our family has had strong political opinions. José Antonio's grandfather served three years in prison. We were *fichado como gusanos* (identified as traitors). We disapproved of the economic system; we wanted to be free. On June 15th, José Antonio and I took a plane to Nicaragua, where we stayed for two days. Then we passed through Honduras, Guatemala, and Mexico, reaching Reynosa, Mexico, on August 8, 2019. We paid a *coyote* (smuggler) US$2,000 to cross the Rio Grande. The *migra* (US Border Patrol) then picked us up, and took us to their headquarters for four days. We were returned to Mexico, and went to the Mexican Consulate for two days. Then we headed on to Matamoros, where we waited in a tent by the Gateway Bridge for two months. While living in the tents, we received help from the volunteer group, *Team Brownsville,* including food twice daily, blankets, nonprescription medicine, and, most importantly, encouragement! *Team Brownsville's* volunteers were our angels. Now I'm here at the Good Neighbor Settlement House waiting to go to Pennsylvania tomorrow by bus. And you know what, Señor Pace? After all of this, I'm six weeks pregnant!

■　■　■

A Better Life

My hometown of five thousand inhabitants is San Juan Chamula, Chiapas, Mexico, along the Guatemalan border. My family of four includes myself, Juan Hernández Santis, twenty-six years old; wife, Francisca, twenty-five years old; and sons, Victor Manuel, three years old, and Juan Hernaldo, three months old. I finished six years of primary school, and became a tenant farmer, growing corn and beans on the two acres I rented.

We have come to the US because I want a better life for my sons. There is so much violence where we live. Despite my limited income, I was threatened if I did not pay a monthly sum. So here we are.

I'm sure you have noticed, Señor Jaime, my wife and I have a real problem with our older son, Victor Manuel. He is so jealous of his younger brother, Juan Hernaldo. He cries and screams for his mother's attention. At times, when she is nursing the baby, he tries to grab her breast so he can suckle. I try to divert his attention, carry him around, read to him, give him crayons for coloring . . . but all without success. He continues to cry and yell for his mama. I am a very patient man, but there are limits to my patience. Do you think he will ever outgrow this character trait?

Seeking a better life, we left Chiapas on August 29, 2019. We had a peaceful trip to Matamoros, Mexico, where we waited two nights and one day at the bridge to Brownsville, Texas. A group of volunteers called *Team Brownsville* surprised and helped us at the bridge with food, clothes, and a tarp against the sun and rain. We really appreciated their help.

When we crossed the bridge, the *migra* (immigration authorities) took us to their headquarters and placed us in the *hielera* (cold storage detention room) where we endured extreme cold, glaring light day and night, and stale baloney sandwiches with chips and beans, as our only food.

On September 4th, we passed through the Brownsville bus station and on to the Good Neighbor Settlement House. Tomorrow we leave for Tampa, Florida, where we'll live with my cousin. I'll take whatever job I can find as we begin to have a better life!

■   ■   ■

For My Daughter

There is no future for my three-year-old daughter, Delal, in Guatemala; therefore, I've come to the US. My name is Gloria Floridalma, twenty-five years old; my husband is a barber, twenty-one years old. I'm a homemaker; I've never had a job outside the house.

On June 14th, Delal and I boarded a bus to leave Guatemala. The trip was very costly. A *coyote* (smuggler) charged us $33,000 Quetzales (approximately US$4,300) for the combined bus and private auto trip to the Rio Grande, near Reynosa, Mexico. Then we paid US$1,500 to cross the river on a large inflatable float, guided by a paddle . . . quite scary!

We walked approximately two hours before the *migra* (border patrol) picked us up near McAllen, Texas. At the *migra* headquarters, we were put in the *hielera* (cold storage detention room) for four days. It was very crowded, so we had to sleep sitting up, eat cold, stale baloney sandwiches, and remain under the intense glare of lights day and night. Little daughter Delal was cold and hungry the entire four days; she cried a lot. They then took us to the detention center in Hidalgo, Texas, for a day. The food was much better: tacos, apples, and milk.

Now we're here at the Good Neighbor Settlement House in Brownsville, Texas, en route to Hyattsville, Maryland. There we'll be living with my father and brother, twenty-nine years old. Both have jobs. I want to learn English and also get a job.

■   ■   ■

For My Son

My name is Lorennza Martínez, a thirty-eight-year-old mother from El Salvador, with only two years of education. I have worked in a tortilla factory for many years. My twenty-one-year-old daughter is an athlete with twelve years of education, and her brother, Kemian, is fourteen years old, with eight years of education.

I am in the US because of Kemian. There are many *pandillas* (gangs) in El Salvador. They not only extort people for money, but even worse—they will kill the young male who refuses to join them, when asked. I wasn't willing to allow Kemian to be in such a situation, so here we are in the US.

On May 13th, we left El Salvador by bus; traveled by auto on the main Mexican highways to Reynosa which cost us approximately US$1,200. We crossed the Rio Grande by launch on May 18th, and were picked up by the *migra* (border patrol) in McAllen, Texas. In the *migra* headquarters, we endured the *hielera* (cold storage detention room) for two days; then we were transferred to El Valle Detention Facility in Raymondville, Texas, for a few days. Once again, we endured the inhumane *hielera* upon arrival and departure.

Now we're here at the Good Neighbor Settlement House in Brownsville, Texas, with a scheduled plane flight to Baltimore, Maryland, on May 25th. We'll stay with my sister who's been in the US for three years. I'll take whatever job I can find, and both Kemian and I are going to work hard to learn English.

■ ■ ■

Threatening My Daughters

I never would have been a Jacobo Árbenz, past president of Guatemala. I'm a working-class man, and have been in the construction industry for the past fifteen years. I'm leaving Guatemala because the *pandillas* (gangs) threatened my fifteen- and sixteen-year-old daughters, if I did not become a member of the *pandillas*.

It was bad enough they hit me up and took part of my pay every Saturday when I got paid. But after two months of being threatened, I decided my girls and I had to leave Guatemala. Otherwise, they would have made sex slaves out of my beautiful precious daughters. So we escaped Guatemala and came to the US. My daughters were released from the detention center within a couple of days, and now they're safe with my parents in Houston. They have just completed enrolling in a Houston high school. I'm so happy for them, and trust that the Lord will be with them for the rest of their lives. Today I'm leaving for Houston to complete our family, and, next week, I'll start looking for a construction job. I'm so grateful.

■ ■ ■

No Hay Trabajo

(There Is No Work)

As a forty-year-old Guatemalan laborer with nine children, I have spent most of my life cutting brush. My name is San Ramiro Vida. I clear around two acres, three days per week, converting scrub to pasture for cattle, or to farmland for agricultural crops. It's nearly impossible to support a family of eleven from the money I receive for three days' work. I have left Guatemala for lack of work.

On April 25, 2019, I left by bus without using a *coyote* (smuggler). I had no problems en route to Reynosa, Mexico, and arrived May 8th. I crossed the Rio Grande by launch, paying only $100 Mexican Pesos, approximately US$5.50. I walked for one-and-a-half hours before the *migra* (border patrol) picked us up. For three days, I was kept in the inhumane *hielera* (cold storage detention room); then, I was transferred to El Valle Detention Center in Raymondville, Texas. I stayed for only one day, but had to endure the *hielera,* once again, upon arriving and leaving.

The next day, I arrived to the Brownsville, Texas, bus station and then went to the Good Neighbor Settlement House. Now I'm ready to go live with a friend in Trenton, New Jersey. I realize it will be very difficult to bring up other family members to join me. I'll take any job I can find, and begin sending part of my pay back to Guatemala to help support my children.

■ ■ ■

Family and Government

RAÚL:

I am a real family man, even though I am a twenty-nine-year-old Cuban bachelor. Growing up, I was encouraged by my mother and dad to do what I wanted to do, and at the same time, to be a responsible human being. Yes, I had lots of fun as a kid, but before I was six, I always had a pencil in my hand, spending hours drawing and drawing not only what I saw, but also what I imagined. Then I started painting, experimenting with different mediums and techniques, finally settling on *acuarela* (watercolor). Contrary to popular opinion, watercolor is more difficult than oil painting. I finished secondary school, but I was self-taught in art. I am most capable of teaching art, but I could never get a job because of my political views and family history.

What a family! What a family history! Presently, already living in Florida are my grandmother, two aunts, a niece, and an evangelical pastor brother. Our family is already working to get my mom and *papi* (father) to the US. For several generations, our family has been persecuted by the Cuban government, despite my great uncle having fought with Fidel and the 26th of July Movement in the *Sierra Maestra* against the Yankee stooge and dictator, [Fulgencio] Batista. He turned his back on the movement, however, because of the deaths and disappearances during the early leadership, the growing corruption in the government, and the blind allegiance to Fidel and the communist credo and practice. He fled Cuba before he was killed.

The government persecution continued to the next generation. One of my uncles was the owner of the independent library *José Oropesa*

Hernández in Havana. The government pressured him for some time to stop selling noncommunist books and magazines. He refused to change, so one morning while on a motorbike with his wife on the outskirts of Havana, they were run over by a speeding government car, which deliberately turned into him.[25] He was lucky to survive the impact, but was crippled for life with his left leg amputated, and his right leg left unusable. Needless to say, the bookstore was closed.

JAMES PACE:

Life continued to be made miserable by the government authorities for all of asylum seeker Raúl's uncles and brothers.

In early fall of 2018, Raúl paid US$8,000 for a place on a launch to Cancún, Mexico. From there, he traveled to the Mexican-Texas border, crossed the bridge seeking asylum in Brownsville, Texas, endured the *hielera* (cold storage detention room) the customary three times, and the Port Isabel Detention Center for forty days. From Brownsville, he's off by bus to Miami, where he'll reunite with all of his family, do what he can to bring his parents to the US . . . for, as always, "it's family first."

■   ■   ■

25 Misceláneas de Cuba. "Agredido el bibliotecario independiente José Ignacio Oropeza Almora." *miscelaneasdecuba.net*, 23 Oct. 2009, http://www.miscelaneasdecuba.net/web/Article/Index/51811f133a682e0f88c4f61c#.XqXGQRY1iEc

John Moore/Getty Images News
BORDER PATROL AGENTS DETAIN MIGRANTS FROM HONDURAS
(MOTHER AND TWO-YEAR-OLD DAUGHTER) NEAR US–MEXICO
BORDER (MCALLEN, TEXAS)
June 12, 2018

Chapter 5

A Woman's Experience

"'Look," said Naomi, "your sister-in-law is going back to her people and her gods. Go back with her." But Ruth replied, "Don't urge me to leave you or to turn back from you. Where you go I will go, and where you stay I will stay. Your people will be my people and your God my God. Where you die I will die, and there I will be buried. May the LORD deal with me, be it ever so severely, if even death separates you and me."

When Naomi realized that Ruth was determined to go with her, she stopped urging her."

RUTH 1:15–18
New International Version (NIV) Bible

Trauma Never Forgotten

Interview conducted, transcribed, and translated by Sandra Milagros
(a pseudonym) Edited by James Pace

SANDRA:

Karen is a pregnant, nineteen-year-old Honduran dropped off at the Brownsville, Texas, bus station early one morning. I introduced myself and the rest of the immigrant support team, taking her trip information and helping her contact her family with my cell phone. While waiting for her parents to call back with her ticket information, Karen and I just chatted. Her uncle in Virginia gave her the information, and she decided to go to the Good Neighbor Settlement House to remain, until her bus departure at 11:30 a.m. the next day.

I drove Karen to the Good Neighbor Settlement House and, right after getting in the car, she started to unload. In a whispery voice, she said, "We were kidnapped and held captive for six days by Mexican policemen." Hugging her just-received backpack, her eyes swelling with tears as she returned my gaze, Karen was just waiting for the right time to pour her heart out to someone. "There were six of us and they beat us and beat us every day, and they gave us so little food, we were starved. They stopped beating me when I bled and told them I was pregnant, but then started torturing me by hitting me with something on my hands. Look!" There were scars all over her hands. She was not raped, but witnessed three of the other girls get raped, including a fourteen-year-old. Finally, she was released by the police after the *coyote* (smuggler) paid the ransom of $10,000.

Karen remembers very little until she awakened in a hospital on this side of the border. The nurses told her she was found unconscious on a river levee by the US Customs and Border Protection agents and brought to the hospital. She doesn't know how many days she was unconscious. Her face was badly bruised and her eyes were nearly swollen shut. Karen saw me crying while telling me her story, but she had the strength to say, "Don't cry. I'm okay."

When we arrived at Good Neighbor, I felt so useless. I felt I had nothing to offer her. I hugged her, showering her with words of encouragement. I made sure she ate, got clean clothes, and showered before I left. Being a Texas Southmost College student, I had to go to class, but asked a colleague to take care of her. Karen was so grateful and could not stop thanking me. I will never forget that look in her eyes—that seemingly sightless stare.

■　■　■

My Twin Soul Sister

JAMES PACE:

Soad Medina is from San Pedro Sula, the most violent and ravaged city in Honduras. ("Soad" in Aramaic means "help, support"). She has a *Licenciatura en Negocios* (business degree), but not at a university level. Her father is a mechanic; she has four siblings.

Soad rode the bus all the way to the US border. A *coyote* (smuggler) led the way, and once getting his group across the Rio Grande, he called the *migra* (border patrol), deserted them, and returned to Mexico. Soad had paid the *coyote* US$6,000 before beginning the trip.

Unfortunately, Soad became infected with ticks all over her body. She was put in isolation and treated for three days to rid the ticks. She was in two other detention centers for five weeks, before being dropped off at the Brownsville bus station. Hurricane Michael [October 2018] delayed her trip to live with her sister in New Orleans, but staying at the Good Neighbor Settlement House was a positive experience. She rested, sang, played with the twenty-nine travelers also stranded with her, ate well, and prepared for the next day's journey to New Orleans.

Soad wants to go to university with a double major in English and philosophy, becoming a professor of these two disciplines. She has a head start in English, after having used tapes in English for several years. During my interview of her, I was impressed with her knowledge of many different topics, her intelligence, and quickness in carrying her part of the conversation. In closing our time together, I told her, *"He encontrado mi gemela de alma en tu persona"* (I have encountered my soul's twin in you).

■　■　■

Maira's Faith

MAIRA:

The trip from Guatemala was hard, traveling both on foot and by bus, sleeping at times under the stars. I could not have made it without help along the way from both old friends and new friends made in Guatemala and Mexico. But most of all, I got help from the Lord Jesus; He sustained me all the way.

You see, I've only believed in Him for the past three years. Until I became a member of a Pentecostal church named *Prince of Peace*, I had hate in my heart for those who discriminated against and oppressed me and my people for being indigenous. Once the Lord Jesus came into my heart, I forgave my oppressors; and through forgiving them, I no longer had hate in my heart. I could live in peace.

JAMES PACE:
And what is your dream to realize once you start living with your sister in New Orleans?

MAIRA:
I want to finish secondary. Then I want to enter a university and study English and theology.

JAMES PACE:
And then, Maira?

MAIRA:
Only the Lord Jesus knows.

■　■　■

Chapter 6

COURAGE

"Meanwhile, the Philistine, with his shield bearer in front of him, kept coming closer to David. He looked David over and saw that he was little more than a boy, glowing with health and handsome, and he despised him. He said to David, 'Am I a dog, that you come at me with sticks?' And the Philistine cursed David by his gods. 'Come here,' he said, 'and I'll give your flesh to the birds and the wild animals!' David said to the Philistine, 'You come against me with sword and spear and javelin, but I come against you in the name of the LORD Almighty, the God of the armies of Israel, whom you have defied. This day the LORD will deliver you into my hands, and I'll strike you down and cut off your head. This very day I will give the carcasses of the Philistine army to the birds and the wild animals, and the whole world will know that there is a God in Israel. All those gathered here will know that it is not by sword or spear that the LORD saves; for the battle is the LORD's, and he will give all of you into our hands.' As the Philistine moved closer to attack him, David ran quickly toward the battle line to meet him. Reaching into his bag and taking out a stone, he slung it and struck the Philistine on the forehead. The stone sank into his forehead, and he fell face down on the ground. So David triumphed over the Philistine with a sling and a stone; without a sword in his hand he struck down the Philistine and killed him."

I Samuel 17:41–50
New International Version (NIV) Bible

What a Woman!

I'm a forty-four-year-old Cuban housewife and mother of daughters, aged eighteen and twenty-one. They both have finished secondary. We are very close and I am very proud of them, having raised them in the small town of Campechuela. I am not going into great detail about my personal or family life; for since they are still in Cuba, I don't want the authorities to punish them, if my words identify me and get back to Cuba. My pseudonym is Rosa Álvarez.

On June 26, 2016, I was among a group of twenty-five (twenty men and five women) who left the port of Mariel, near Havana, in a motorized boat at night. Remember the so-called *Marielitos* (Mariel Cubans) who flooded Miami by the thousands in 1980, among whom Fidel Castro mixed inmates of several prisons and patients from mental hospitals? We thought we were also going to Miami, but not far from shore we were intercepted by a Cuban patrol boat and escorted back to Mariel.

Jailed for seventy-two hours, we were called *gusanos* (counter-revolutionaries) and *cínicos* (cynics), worthless of living in Cuba. One of my fingers was put in a vise and twisted for around thirty minutes. Look at how crooked it is now. We were warned upon being released that we would be in prison for a long time, if we again violated the law.

I then went home and for a year took care of my mother who had suffered a heart attack. During that time, I joined the Cuban Methodist Church in Manzanillo. It proved to be a real blessing in my life. In March, 2018, I went to Trinidad and Tobago as a tourist and stayed for six months. I took enough merchandise with me to net US$500 in sales, but upon returning to Cuba, the authorities confiscated all my earnings. I had to pay a fine for throwing a bucket of water on the sidewalk in front of my home, in protest of their robbing me.

On October 10, 2018, I attended a cousin's *quinceañera* (coming-out party for girls who have reached their fifteenth birthday). I gave a speech on the history of slavery in Cuba. It was considered a political statement. Someone at the party told the police, and, once again, I was picked up. This time they pulled one of my teeth, and threatened if there were a next time, most likely, I would disappear.

I had had enough. I had to leave. I signed a contract with a Mexican company to go and work as a sales consultant in Cancún, Mexico. After flying there, I forgot about my contract, and took a bus straight to Matamoros and crossed the Los Tomates bridge into Brownsville, Texas, without the use of a *coyote* (smuggler) the entire trip. Immigration sent me to the Port Isabel Detention Center where I was held for forty-five days. So here I am in the Brownsville bus station ready to go live in Seguin, Texas, with my sister.

It's rather symbolic, I think, to come from the land of Jose Martí, hero of the fight for Cuban independence from Spain, to the town named after Colonel Juan Seguín, one of the heroes of the fight for Texas independence from Mexico.

■　■　■

Mighty Mouse

I am Martín Villanueva, from a village of nine hundred inhabitants, some thirty kilometers from San Pedro Sula [Honduras], a region known for its violence. Extortion and robbery are everyday occurrences. On July 10th last year, I was accosted on the street, and two bad guys took my cell phone. I denounced them to the police, but they did nothing. Our justice system is so corrupt; two *pistoleros* (gunmen) killed a judge, and in two weeks they were walking free in the plaza. In 2018, law enforcement got worse and worse.

Many people consider me a shrimp; I am soft-spoken, weigh 110 pounds and am 5' 5" tall. Bullies think they can push me around, but I stand up to them and stand my ground. I've had several shirts badly torn, but I'm not going to give in to being pushed around.

I have a technical professional degree in accounting, and was working in a hardware store. For four months last year, a group of *maleantes* (gangsters) were pressuring me to give them names and addresses of other employees, how we did our banking, when we had the most cash in the store, and where we might have any hidden. Finally, on October 29th, one of the *maleantes* jammed a pistol into my stomach, and told me I soon would be dead, if I didn't tell them what they wanted to know in a couple of days. I knew I couldn't hide in Honduras because there's an organized crime ring in my country.

My mother said, "Go, Son." My father had abandoned my mother and me when I was only eight months old. So I took a bus through all of Central America and Mexico, and crossed the *Río Bravo* (Rio Grande) on a raft for 300 Mexican Pesos [US$12.50]. After I walked for an hour, the *migra* (border patrol) spotted me, put me in their van, and then in the *hielera* (cold storage detention room) for four days. I wore only a T-shirt, and slept in a sitting position because there were so many people in the *hielera*. We had only cold baloney sandwiches to eat.

Transferred to El Valle Detention Facility in Raymondville, Texas, the forty days I was there were okay. I paid my bond of US$1,500.00, and here I am in Brownsville.

I'm going to live with my aunt in Baltimore, Maryland. I'll get a job fairly quickly because there's always need for an honest accountant. One thing is certain: I may be soft-spoken and small, but I'm not going to be pushed around by anybody.

■   ■   ■

A Hard-fought Struggle

Interview of "JC" by Andrea Rudnik, Team Brownsville
Supplemental Interview of "JC" by James Pace

ANDREA RUDNIK:

I met "JC" at the Brownsville bus station on Saturday morning. He arrived there from the Port Isabel Detention Center, along with a group of fifteen other men who had been released to reunite with their loved ones throughout the country. "JC" had a broad smile, and looked like he was ready to tell his story. He sat down with me, holding a large pile of papers and documents and began the saga. He spoke to me in Spanish, and showed me many supporting documents from people in Nicaragua who knew him and attested to what he had been involved with, while living in Nicaragua. Here's his story, in my translation from Spanish to English.

"JC":

I'm from a small city in Nicaragua called La Trinidad. I'm a hardworking man with a wife and child. My city has become a hotbed of political activity, as the people in power, the Sandinistas, threaten the lives of those of us who oppose them. I was a taxi driver, and my life was threatened and my work was taken from me, because I don't support the human rights violations by the Sandinista party. I participated in marches and sit-ins to say, "No, we will not stand for people's livelihoods and their lives being taken from them, because they do not support this communist regime." I participated in the last electoral process and was targeted by the current ruler of Nicaragua, for opposing his party and policies.

Once I realized I had to leave my beloved Nicaragua, I collected documentation, which I knew I would need to plead my asylum case in the United States. I didn't really know what it was going to take to be given asylum, but I was determined to succeed. I left my wife and beautiful daughter there, not knowing when or if I would see them again. It was very difficult to leave them.

I traveled for many days on buses, passing through El Salvador, Honduras, Guatemala, and Mexico, before reaching the border at Reynosa. When we reached Reynosa, our bus was stopped by armed men who told us to get out. Then we were asked if we were going to the United States. Those of us who said "Yes" were separated from the others. These armed men told us they were members of the *** Cartel and would cross us into the United States, in return for a large sum of money. Most of us had heard about this and were prepared to pay all our life savings for a chance to go to the United States. The truth is we weren't given any options, and those that didn't have enough money disappeared from the group before we crossed. We didn't want to think about what happened to them.

We were crossed in a shallow part of the river, forced to crouch down and wait for four days, surrounded by mosquitoes buzzing around our heads, and freezing water encircling our bodies. My whole body swelled up, and I couldn't feel my arms and legs anymore. The armed men had bales of drugs with them, which they crossed with us, about twenty men in all.

Finally, we were given the signal to come out of the water. I could barely walk and my head was spinning. I'm diabetic, and I hadn't eaten all that time, so my blood sugar must have been really low.

We were put into a van and driven away from the river to I don't know where. At some point, we were forced out of the van and told to walk. The van sped off into the distance, leaving our group standing there with nothing but the clothes on our backs. We just started walking and walking. Some time later, the US Border Patrol apprehended me, and I asked for asylum. I was actually happy to see them, because I was thirsty and starving, and felt like I was going to die. I remember the name Falfurrias—that's where we were taken.

I was processed through CBP [US Customs and Border Protection], and spent eleven days in the *hielera*—that freezing cold room with no windows, just hard concrete floors and benches, plus a bright light overhead that was on day and night. Once I finished my credible fear paperwork, I was sent to the Port Isabel Detention Center, where I've been the last four months.

I fought and fought my case there, because I didn't have any money to pay a bond to get out. Attorneys from ProBAR [South Texas Pro Bono Asylum Representation Project], who help people like me fight their case, assisted me. They helped me so much, and researched my case, my city and my country's history, so they would know what I've been through.

I almost got deported a week or so back, but then I got my miracle. The judge who reviewed my case said to me: "You are the kind of person asylum was made for; you have demonstrated you did the right thing; you show credible fear in your story; you are a man of your word; you have no criminal record. You are hereby granted asylum."

I have strong faith in Jesus Christ and He has carried me through this. Without Jesus, I'm nothing. I can't believe you volunteers are here to greet us. We weren't expecting anyone to be happy to see us, much less offer us breakfast, backpacks, and clothing.

ANDREA RUDNIK:
The end of the story for "JC" hasn't come yet. He's full of life and hope for the future. He got to speak to his wife and daughter for the first time in four months through a *#TeamBrownsville* volunteer's phone and WhatsApp. *Team Brownsville* was also able to help pay for his bus ticket

to Miami, since he came out of detention with no money. He's a man of great faith and hopes he will be able to reunite with his family soon.

JAMES PACE:
Living in the town of La Trinidad, province of Estelí, Nicaragua, became impossible for "JC" by the fall of 2018. On August 28, 2018, the Sandinista government issued an official order accusing him of "Terrorism, Organized Crime, Obstruction of Public Service, and Holding Clandestine, Illegal Meetings in Subject's House with Subversive Intent."

In spite of the fact "JC" claims the accusation was one big fat lie, he had to take it very seriously. "JC" recounts how his friend had been arrested and tortured, including the crushing, maiming, and mutilation of his body—treatment worse than death, in "JC's" opinion.

"JC" comments that from April, 2018, to the end of 2018, over one thousand citizens have been killed by the Nicaraguan government, and another one thousand have mysteriously disappeared. "JC" asks me: "What chance did I have of surviving, if I remained in my homeland?"

"JC" says he did not wait for his government's published edict. He had previously taken steps to defend himself, as he realized he had been identified in the protest marches and sit-ins. He first received a written declaration from the mayor, Bismarck Antonio Rayo Gámez, as to his character and good conduct as a citizen of La Trinidad. Then he had asked for and received an official letter of support from the Bishop Juan Abelardo Mata Guevara of Estelí province. (The Bishop is recognized as being opposed to the Sandinista government's abuses). The Bishop's letter was directed to the Commission on Human Rights in the capital city, Managua. "JC" delivered the letter personally to the Commission, and received a letter of his rights as a human being. At first while assembling these letters, he felt they would defend him against the government, but just a few days passed before he knew all the letters in the world would not protect him against the bestiality of the Sandinistas. But yes, his supporting statements and the government proclamation against him would prove he had a credible fear of death, a requirement for asylum in the US.

"JC" came by train through Mexico to Reynosa, and crossed the border with the help of the cartel; he was finally caught and taken to the Falfurrias, Texas, border patrol station and checkpoint on US Highway 281. From there, he was taken to the Port Isabel Detention Center where he received full asylum from the immigration judge, for which he is eternally grateful. He describes spending four months in detention as abominable, but that's behind him now. He's happy and eager to join family in Miami.

It was interesting to note that while having lunch with seven other released detainees and four of us volunteers, "JC" talked incessantly, smiled, and enjoyed his taco, enchilada, beans and rice; but most of all, he exclaimed repeatedly his simple delight in the sweetened black coffee . . . *delicioso* (delicious). He had three cups of coffee. He explains, *"Por cuatro meses, no he tenido ni café, ni azúcar; no nos dieron ni una sola taza de café."* (For four months, I have had neither coffee nor sugar; they didn't give us one single cup of coffee).

■ ■ ■

I Swam Across

I am a single fourth-year medical student from Camagüey, Cuba. My name is Ángel Aenlle. I received an excellent medical education from Carlos J. Finlay University of Medical Sciences of Camagüey. Even though my family had spent twenty-three years in opposition to the Cuban government, I knew better than to express my political opinions in public. Consequently, I never had any trouble with the police.

With my family's long history of opposition to the government, I knew my time was short before the government would put me in the same political boat as my family. So, in spite of postponing my last year of medical studies, on June 12, 2019, I left by plane to Nicaragua. My expenses included a visa for US$30, taxis US$130, and a Honduras safe conduct letter for US$180. I took the bus to Guatemala and through all of Mexico, reaching Matamoros, Mexico, on July 12th. There I stayed in a church-sponsored migrant house for five days. Not wanting to join other asylum seekers waiting weeks and months to cross the bridge to the US, I swam across the Rio Grande River on July 17th, and was immediately detained by the *migra* (border patrol). They transferred me to their headquarters in McAllen, and put me in the *hielera* (cold storage detention room) where I endured all of its inhumane treatment for twelve days.

On July 29th, they transferred me to El Valle Detention Facility in Raymondville, Texas. My treatment there was okay, and I left El Valle on October 28th for the Port Isabel Detention Center near Los Fresnos, Texas, a stark contrast to El Valle. Port Isabel was like a prison, with double lines of concertina wire, frequent roll call, and demeaning treatment by many of the guards. I was really glad when I got out of there early this morning, December 4th.

So here I am at Good Neighbor Settlement House, preparing to take the bus to Miami, Florida, where I'll be living with a large family of grandparents, uncles, aunts, and cousins. As soon as I arrange my papers, I'll finish my fifth and final year of medical studies, and fulfill my dream of being a doctor!

■   ■   ■

I'm Not My Dad

My name is Pascual Díaz, a twenty-three-year-old male from Chiapas, Mexico. My wife is Cecilia, twenty-five years old, and our son, José David, eight months old. Our son is quite a pistol—very active, interested in everything and everyone, including strangers sitting across the table from him. Right now, he constantly is trying to open the zipper on a plastic bag. We've been told all of this behavior indicates a high degree of intelligence.

My family owns an acre of land on which we grow corn, beans, and squash. Nearly all our harvest goes to feed us; we are subsistence farmers. However, in spite of our apparent poverty, over the years my father had accumulated a lot of money. He consequently loaned much of it to neighbors and others in Chiapas. When my dad died, his debtors expected me as the eldest son to continue dad's practice of lending them money. However, I'm not my dad, and I refused to lend them anymore. My action caused them to threaten me, saying, "Continue to bankroll us, or suffer the consequences!"

So here we are in the US. We're going to Kentucky, where a friend has a restaurant. I'll either get into agriculture, or one day have my own restaurant. I want to thank you, Señor Pace, for indicating how to speed up learning English by buying English tapes and repeating them over and over, as a child does with *mamá* (mother) and *agua* (water).

■　■　■

UNDOCUMENTED IMMIGRANTS ARE LED AFTER BEING
HANDCUFFED BY BORDER PATROL AGENTS
Weslaco, Texas, April 2016
John Moore/Getty Images

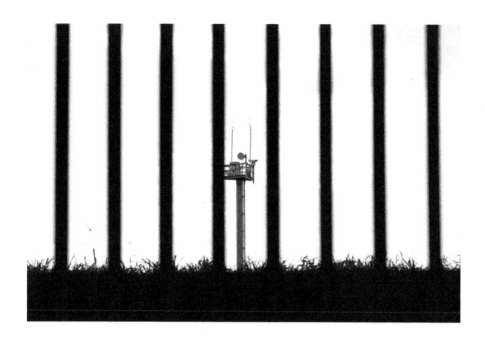

Antony Pace Farias © 2017
BROWNSVILLE, TEXAS, BORDER WALL AND WATCHTOWER
ALONG OLD MILITARY HIGHWAY
2017

"Not like the brazen giant of Greek fame,
With conquering limbs astride from land to land;
Here at our sea-washed, sunset gates shall stand
A mighty woman with a torch, whose flame
Is the imprisoned lightning, and her name
Mother of Exiles."

Excerpt from "The New Colossus"
by Emma Lazarus

Chapter 7

US RECEPTION

"Enter his gates with thanksgiving and his courts with praise; give thanks to him and praise his name. For the LORD is good and his love endures forever; his faithfulness continues through all generations."

PSALM 100:4–5
New International Version (NIV) Bible

"Upon arriving to the US, I never expected to be so mistreated by her government's authorities."
—*Honduran Asylum Seeker*

Refugee Encounter

JAMES PACE:

Let me describe a personal encounter I had with a refugee this past Saturday. Four of us from the First United Methodist Church and Good Neighbor Settlement House in Brownsville, Texas, were sitting in the local bus station at 5:30 a.m. We were awaiting the immigration authorities to drop off two van loads of twenty-six refugees from the Port Isabel Detention Center. At 6:15 a.m., here they came through the bus station's double doors. They were tired and hungry; they were awake all night while being processed; the *migra* (immigration) didn't even give them a cup of coffee or a tortilla. And here they were for us to help.

We gave the refugees backpacks with nonperishable food, sweat-shirts, etc. to protect them from the cold on the buses, loaned them our cell phones to call their relatives in the US, interpreted their bus tickets and fielded many questions such as: 'Where are we? How long will it take to reach my destination?'

Among this group was Héctor Chávez from Guatemala. He was flying to Boston to live with his uncle. I told him I would take him to the Brownsville/South Padre Island International Airport, but he would have to wait until we finished helping all of his companions. Then I drove Héctor and three others to the Good Neighbor Settlement House for breakfast, and from there, he and I headed for the airport.

En route, Héctor Chávez began questioning me.

HÉCTOR CHÁVEZ:
Who are all of you?

JAMES PACE:
We're mainly members of the Evangelical Methodist Church of America.

HÉCTOR CHÁVEZ:
Methodist. Are there Methodists in Guatemala?

JAMES PACE:
Yes, there are three different Methodist churches in Guatemala.

HÉCTOR CHÁVEZ:
Why are you doing this?

JAMES PACE:
For the love of Jesus in our hearts; He taught us to help our neighbor in need.

(When I had parked my car in front of the departure gate):
HÉCTOR CHÁVEZ:
Give me your postal address and telephone number.

JAMES PACE:
Why do you want them?

HÉCTOR CHÁVEZ:
Well, I want to stay in contact, and I want to send you some money, so I can help you continue to aid those coming after me.

(After exchanging addresses, we got out of the car and I walked over to him. He faced me, looked me in the eye):

'Mr. Pace,' putting his closed fist over his heart, 'I will always keep you in my heart for all the love you have given me.'

JAMES PACE:
And I will always keep Héctor Chávez from Guatemala in my heart. As Bishop Sante Uberto Barbieri used to say, 'dije,' . . . 'I've said it.'

■ ■ ■

I'm Sorry

JAMES PACE:

What would lead an immigration judge to tell a detainee upon releasing him from the Port Isabel Detention Center: "I'm sorry"?

"I'm sorry" for your unnecessary stay here of three months, for your having your freedom taken away from you: your freedom to be with family and friends in Mexico; your freedom to work on a ranch near Lubbock, Texas, or to obtain a well-paying construction job in the Dallas area, instead of US$1.00 per day for ten hours of peeling potatoes; your freedom to go where you want to, when you want to.

"I'm sorry" for what you have suffered and endured these ninety days in the intensely cold and cramped quarters, where you had to sleep sitting up under the glare of unyielding lights in the *hielera* (cold storage detention room), eat cold, often half-frozen, baloney sandwiches, listen to and empathize with the childrens' suffering from hunger and cold, submit to the discipline of a two-hour countdown, pay for commissary items at three times their market value, wonder daily when you would be released from this unjust detention.

"I'm sorry" for your unlawful detention, for it was brought to my attention that you, Jaime Paz (a pseudonym), have been a legal resident of the United States since 1988, thirty-one years. How could that have occurred? Well, your record shows you were accused of trying to smuggle arms into Mexico on your last of many trips to visit your family in Guanajuato. We now understand this was a setup by Mexican authorities to squeeze you out of everything you had: money, personal possessions, and a car. You protested you were clean and not guilty of any crime, but your protests were futile. Once on your record, upon your return to the US on the Hidalgo, Texas, bridge, you were wrongfully taken into custody, and have endured suffering these past ninety days.

Unfortunately, Señor Paz, the only consolation I can give you is, "I'm sorry."

■　■　■

Gratitude

"I can't believe what I'm seeing," stated a graying, robust Cuban man in his forties one early morning at the Brownsville, Texas, bus station. "All you people showering us with needed items, from shoelaces and belts to backpacks filled with food, clothes, and blankets. What a surprise it will be for my family left in Cuba, when I write them."

Surveying all the activity around him, this asylum seeker then exclaimed, "Look over here! Your compadre has not only explained to and written out the entire itinerary of this woman's bus ticket, but, now, he is tracing her travel route on a map of the United States from city to city, highlighting where she's going to change buses."

He shakes his head, smiles, and then asserts, "When we first entered the bus station, you greeted us with smiles, words of welcome, and then we heard, 'We are here to help you; whatever you need we can provide, just ask us.' Then you offered us the use of your cell phones to call our relatives at our final destination, free of charge!" He paused, looked down for a moment, and then looked directly at me. He proclaimed, "You have done much more than what you promised. You're our angels."

■   ■   ■

My Horror Story

LÁZARO:

My name is Lázaro González García (a pseudonym). My pregnant wife and I left Cuba on June 9th, flying to French Guiana, and from there through Brazil and eleven other countries by bus and on foot to get to the US border. Going through jungle, desert, plains, and mountains was rough at times, but the only real trouble we had was in Nicaragua. We were jailed for three weeks for being "traitors to the Cuban Revolution," but after paying our fines and more, we were permitted to continue northward.

We arrived to the Matamoros-Brownsville border on September 6th, but had to wait our turn of three people daily entering the US. We lived under the Mexico-Texas railroad bridge for ten days. As soon as we crossed to the US, we were slapped into *la hielera*, (cold storage detention room), where I was kept for two days, and my wife for only one day because of her pregnancy. The *hielera* was in the middle of the main bridge's immigration building, and extremely cold. Without blankets, we slept on the floor, ate cold, stale bologna sandwiches twice daily, and our drinking water came from the lavatory basin.

I then was transferred to the Port Isabel Detention Center, but due to a lack of space, I was part of a group transferred to El Valle Detention Facility, forty-five miles away. Some of us were so upset by our detainment we started banging our heads against the cell doors; the horrors began. I saw a dead man. I asked to see a psychologist. My jailers' answer? They took away all my clothes, threw me into a solitary cell measuring 1.5 x 1.5 meters, and provided no food or water for four days. 'Nothing for commies!' They later told me they had been afraid of my committing suicide.

Placed back in the general population, I found there was nothing to do. We protested and were allowed to play cards and shoot dice— only games of the guards' choosing. Every three hours, we stood at attention by our beds to be counted; lights out at ten. Talking was prohibited after ten; talking heard? . . . lights back on for an hour. Silence. I was permitted weekly telephone calls to my wife, now in Miami. Once, they allowed me to call my mother. That was the only contact we had with the outside world for forty to sixty days—no information about anything.

When we entered El Valle, we were told to hand over our money, and we could draw on it for personal necessities. Most of us had US$10–$50.00 on account, but when we tried to withdraw some of our money, we were told, '*Ya no hay.*' (There is none now). We asked, 'What happened to my money?' They responded, 'We don't know.' Medicines had the same fate. 'Hand them over; we'll get you some replacements.'

When we asked, 'Where is the medicine I need?', they countered, 'We don't have any.' What's more is there were five cellmates in quarantine where I was living. I was returned to solitary confinement for twenty-nine days. Why? I don't know. The guards tried to humiliate us constantly: laughing at you as they pushed your food through the slot in the door; creating a bugle-like sound to torment you day and night. Two weeks after leaving solitary, a psychologist approached me, 'How are you doing?'

I wanted out of detention, so I replied: 'Oh, I'm doing much better now; I'm not having any further nervous attacks.' I wasn't going to give him any reason to keep me in any longer.

Now that I'm out, I know I'm carrying the psychological wounds of my captivity. In the last twenty-four hours, my stomach hurts, I can't sleep, loud sounds scare me, I start sweating and can't stand to remain in a closed room, nor do I want to be close to anyone representing authority or who is bossy. I know I'm sick and need a psychologist.

El Valle Detention Facility was my well of despair. At thirty-four years old, I was crying like a baby, after being there for three days. Never have I suffered so much in my life, including when I lost my dad. Not one day of traveling through deserts and jungle compared to one day in detention. For me, El Valle was equivalent psychologically to a World War II Nazi concentration camp.

Where am I going and what are my dreams? I'm headed to West Palm Beach, Florida, to be with my thirteen- and fourteen-year-old sons, my pregnant wife, and to await the birth of our child in four months.

I am a good carpenter, a master in my craft. I will have no trouble getting a good job. I need a good psychologist to help me live through and recover from all of these horrific experiences. No, I have never been a church member.

JAMES PACE:
We had finished the interview, and were sitting in my car with the doors open and all the windows down in the parking lot of Good Neighbor Settlement House in Brownsville, Texas—a place where Lázaro would not feel confined and hemmed in. I reached over to shake his hand. He looked at me, shaking my hand, and said, 'You are the first person to extend me a welcoming hand since coming to America.'

■　■　■

Five Months in Detention

CRISTIAN:

My name is Cristian González (a pseudonym). I am twenty-two years old, from San Juan Ostuncalco, Guatemala. I'm a mechanic, a good mechanic. When I get to California, specifically, the agricultural sector, I won't have trouble finding a job because, as you know, someone always needs a good mechanic. My father has worked for years in a cement block factory. Now, a couple of my ten brothers and sisters are starting to work there also.

You ask why I left a good job in Guatemala? Well, it was either leave or be killed. Several armed men approach you and say, 'We know where you and your big family live. Either join up with us, or we'll kill you.' So here I am in the United States.

My father made all the arrangements for me to leave. He paid US$ 2,000 to the *coyote* (smuggler) to get me to the border; then he was to pay US$3,000 to get me to Houston, half on crossing the border, and half on arriving to Houston.

JAMES PACE:
How were you to get to Houston?

CRISTIAN:
In a trailer truck, an eighteen-wheeler.

JAMES PACE:
Comfortable riding in the trailer with refrigeration?

CRISTIAN:
I wasn't put in the trailer. I was stuffed in the driver's sleeper cab with thirty-four others, men and women. It was so uncomfortable, not only because of being packed in, but there was very little air pushed through by the machine.

JAMES PACE:
Wow! What an experience! How did you get caught?

CRISTIAN:
At a checkpoint, and then back to Laredo to be jailed for four months. I had to be a witness in the court trial against the smuggler. It was a long wait before the trial began. I was in contact with my dad, and he got a lawyer to make sure my rights were protected. Finally, the trial was over.

JAMES PACE:
And then you were released.

CRISTIAN:
Oh, no! Then I was transferred from Laredo to the Port Isabel Detention Center.

JAMES PACE:
Were you disappointed?

CRISTIAN:
A little bit, but I knew I had to clear the *migra* (immigration), and it wasn't so bad there in the detention center. I knew it couldn't be as bad as the four months spent in Laredo. There was less worry now. And I have a whole bunch of cousins to live among in California. So the month flew by, and I'm out now. I can't wait to get to California!

■　■　■

An Emotional Time

Email from James Pace to goddaughter Jennifer Gelwick-Luecke
January, 2019

Doing fine . . . after four consecutive days of 4:00 a.m. get-ups and going to the bus station to greet and help the asylum seekers by 5:30 a.m., I slept in this morning and missed SS [Sunday School], and only made worship at 11:00 a.m.

On Monday, the judges at the detention centers have their preliminary hearings. The asylum seekers have to pay their bonds from 1K to 500K [USD $1,000 to $500,000] for one Chinese several months ago . . . then they are released to our bus station Tuesday–Thursday (Cubans are beginning to be more numerous than Hondureños and Guatemaltecos, with Nicaragüenses now fourth, and Venezolanos beginning to trickle in . . . (Brasileños tapering off, due to government change?).

It's so exhilarating to witness a group of Cubans just released to meet other Cubans in the bus station previously released . . . this happened Saturday. Shouts, laughter, rapid-fire Spanish—loud and simultaneous from different Cubans—happiness, smiles, and back-breaking thumps of hugs (*abrazos fuertes*) . . . I wanted to cry for joy for their happiness, but would only smile for the emotional release of these ten adult Cubans.

Thus is my blessing for working with my refugee brothers and sisters.

■   ■   ■

What Role Models!

My name is Denis Hernández, a twenty-eight-year-old Cuban. I've worked all my life helping to support my parents and two younger brothers. First, I started and developed my own business—a bicycle repair shop. Then, I was a taxi driver with my two-seater bicycle taxi. Certain times each year, I was a tractor driver, mainly driving in manioc and corn fields. Now here in the US, I still remain very active contributing to the common good.

It took time and effort to get to the US. On July 21, 2018, along with twenty-five other Cubans, I left Cuba in the darkness of night in a launch for a two-day trip to Cancún, Mexico. I had to stay in Cancún until September 1st when my house was finally sold. That sale paid for the US$10,000 launch fare and the plane ticket to Reynosa, Mexico. I crossed the border to Hidalgo, Texas, and sought asylum.

Instead of a 'Welcome to the US,' I was thrust into the *hielera* (cold storage detention room) and kept there for eleven days, wearing only a T-shirt, sleeping on a thin plastic sheet on the floor, and eating cold, stale baloney sandwiches twice daily. I was transferred to the Port Isabel Detention Center on September 12th where I was held until released on December 27th. It was tough going at first, but then I got jobs painting the kitchen and then working there for a dollar a day. I also had to endure the *hielera* for two days on entering the Port Isabel Detention Center, and for another twelve hours before being taken to the Brownsville, Texas, bus station. I ask myself, 'Why do the authorities put us in the *hielera* so often? . . . To dissuade other asylum seekers from coming to the US? To intimidate us, cause great fear, to make it easier to control us? Or, is it because they're just plain mean?'

All these experiences are behind me now. I'm presently living in Brownsville, Texas, with two magnificent role models who bonded me out of the detention center: Sergio Cordova and Mike Benavides. Along with me, they are helping two more Cuban brothers. They both have very responsible jobs with the Brownsville Independent School District. Additionally, they spend time on Facebook cultivating financial and material support for backpacks, nonperishable food kits, clothing, shoe-laces, belts, gloves, and cold-weather caps for their work with asylum seekers at the Brownsville, Texas, bus station five mornings weekly. Then, they take hot food, blankets, and tarps across the Rio Grande to those in Matamoros, Mexico, waiting to cross as asylum seekers. Sergio and Mike are my role models.

With them as my role models, I'm committed to helping my two younger brothers to the US, and other asylum seekers after me, know-ing all the time God is helping me.

■   ■   ■

Inhuman Treatment

JAMES PACE:

Attractive, olive skin with dark shoulder-length hair, and a smile which disappeared when she began to tell her story . . . and what a story! María Roca (a pseudonym), forty years old, three-and-a-half-months pregnant, from Honduras, was determined to share all of it, in spite of her tears.

On January 31st, she was taken by the US Border Patrol to the Port Isabel Detention Center for asylum seekers. She stated she did not know what to expect upon arrival at the detention center, and was shocked by what she encountered. She was thrust into the *hielera* (cold storage detention room), wearing only blue jeans and a thin, cotton blouse. The *hielera* was very crowded, with seven children all five years old or younger, and eleven women, mostly pregnant. There were no blankets; everyone slept on thin plastic sheets. There were only cold, stale, baloney sandwiches to eat three times a day, with a little tofu occasionally at supper. Most of the children were crying from hunger and cold.

María and the other women who were pregnant lived in constant fear. Just the previous week, a pregnant woman in the *hielera* had miscarried her three-month-old fetus. All the women felt the death had been caused by the extreme cold. The remaining mothers lived with the question: 'Will my child suffer the same fate?' María endured living with that question for four days, until her release on February 4th. She was brought by ICE personnel [US Immigration and Customs

Enforcement] to the bus station in Brownsville, Texas. Her last words in our interview were: "*Ese tratamiento de nosotros en la hielera fué muy inhumana!*" (That treatment of us in the cold storage detention room was very inhuman!).

■ ■ ■

ACLU of Texas

Email to Michael Seifert,
Policy & Advocacy Strategist

American Civil Liberties Union, ACLU of Texas, February 2019

This is the latest interview regarding the *hielera* . . . cold box.
Date of Interview: February 12, 2019 at Brownsville Texas Municipal
bus station by James Pace of Letty R. from Sulaco, Honduras, age 18

M s. R. arrived at the Port Isabel Detention Center on December 29, 2019. She was placed in the *hielera* [cold storage detention room] upon arrival for eight days. It was very crowded, with approximately forty persons, some four to five children crying from the cold and hunger. She was detained for forty-eight days. Before release, she was in the *hielera* again for ten hours. She was released with fifteen women.

She traveled by bus to Dallas, Texas, to live with her aunt. [Address deleted]. She is both willing and wants to be interviewed; she, too, heard of the tragedy of the mother losing her fetus while in the *hielera*.

■ ■ ■

Why the Cold Storage
Detention Room?

¿Por qué la hielera?

ORLAY RODRÍGUEZ:

Orlay Rodríguez is my name, a forty-four-year-old Cuban. I come from a province of Cuba which covers 10 x 90 kilometers, and has about one hundred forty thousand inhabitants. I finished my twelve years of high school, my favorite subject being math. I took a course in refrigeration, but for the last fifteen years I have worked as a baker and a veterinarian. My wife and I have four children—three boys and a girl, ages four, six, thirteen, and twenty-three.

Since my mother and brother are already in the US, the police *me han fichado como un gusano* (they have identified me as a traitor to the Cuban Revolution). I don't belong to any opposition cell, but I certainly don't agree with the policies or practices of the Cuban government.

I flew to Panama on February 23, 2019, to buy items for my business. The same day I left, I took a bus to Costa Rica. When I got to Nicaragua, I needed several days to get a visa which cost me US$150. I then traveled by bus through Honduras, Guatemala, and Mexico without any problems, arriving in Reynosa, Mexico, on April 30, 2019, where I spent three months in the Evangelical Church, *Sendero de la Vida* (Path of Life). On July 24th, I crossed the bridge over the Rio Grande to McAllen, Texas, where I was taken to the headquarters of the *migra* (US Border Patrol). There I was put in the *hielera* (cold storage detention room) for two days where I suffered extreme cold wearing a T-shirt; was subjected to intense glaring light 24/7; it was so crowded everyone had to sleep standing up; and our daily ration was three burritos (refried beans in three tortillas). Really an inhumane situation of torture.

So I ask you, Señor Pace, 'Why does the US Government use this inhumane, torturous system of the *hielera* on us inoffensive asylum seekers?'

JAMES PACE:
In my opinion, *hermano* Orlay (brother Orlay), the authorities want to show you they're in control, and create such fear resulting from your treatment that word will get back to your countries to dissuade others from following you and seeking asylum. Many of the top US authorities don't want you here; they only want to admit White professionals with money from Europe.

ORLAY RODRÍGUEZ:
After my two days at the McAllen *migra* (immigration) headquarters, I was taken to El Valle Detention Facility in Raymondville, Texas. There I spent ninety days, with more time in the *hielera* on arrival and departure. In spite of the *hielera*, the overall treatment at El Valle was good; the only exception was the food. On October 24th, I left the detention center and was passed through the Brownsville bus station and on to the Good Neighbor Settlement House. At 10:00 p.m. tonight, I'll leave on the Greyhound for Phoenix, Arizona, where I'll live with my brother, and with a job as a chauffeur in his company.

■   ■   ■

My Welcome to America

I am a forty-year-old master industrial welder from Nicaragua. My pseudonym is José Rolveda Rojas. I finished my fourth year in a secondary public school, and am insisting that my three daughters who are twenty, sixteen, and twelve surpass their father in formal education. I joined the protests of the elderly and students against the Sandinista government from the beginning, in April of 2018. The Sandinistas exercise absolute control over the population. Forget about a democratic process—there is no hope for change, at present. To illustrate the severity and inhumane measures they will take, go visit the charred remains of a wooden house four blocks north of the *rótulo* (traffic circle) of the *Virgen María* (Virgin Mary) in Managua. There the authorities surrounded the home of a family identified as leaders of the antigovernment protests, and burned it to the ground with all the inhabitants inside—men, women, and children. That happened April 29th or 30th, 2018.

There was no way I could stay in Nicaragua, so on September 7, 2018, I left Managua by bus for Guatemala. Arriving at the border with Mexico, I crossed the Usumacinta River by launch and headed to Villahermosa, Tabasco, where I was detained by Mexican immigration officials for sixteen days. In Villahermosa, I did receive a humanitarian visa issued by Mexico. I came across the old railroad bridge leading to Brownsville, Texas, and was treated well. Frequently, I was asked by the *migra* (immigration officials), 'Why did you leave Nicaragua'? They didn't seem to be satisfied with my answer. Finally, on December 29th, I was taken to the Port Isabel Detention Center.

You ask me how was life in the Port Isabel Detention Center? *Pésima!* (Nightmarish!).

Life was better in the Nicaraguan jails than the Port Isabel Detention Center. Here are my complaints, substantiated by other asylum seekers:

- drinking water has so much chlorine, it burns your throat as you swallow;

- drinking water is passed through the *caldera* (boiler) before you get to drink it;

- food is the same, day after day—milk and dry cereal for breakfast; cold, stale baloney sandwiches for lunch; baloney sandwiches, sometimes only bread and a little tofu, plus an apple for supper;

- supper is served at 4:00 p.m. and breakfast at 6:00 a.m.;

- when we are delivered to the Brownsville, Texas, bus station starting at 5:00 a.m. and lasting until 11:00 a.m., our last meal was served at 4:00 p.m. the previous day;

- the commissary is run like an enrichment business with exorbitant price gouging; prices are tripled; a small coke is US$1.75;

- compare that to the daily detainee's wage of US$1.00 for peeling potatoes for ten hours;

- countdown every two hours;

- dirty hand towels to wash up with;

- four *hieleras, pozos,* (cold storage detention rooms) (wells, holes), very cold, no cold weather clothes allowed, bright lights shining twenty-four hours, sometimes held ten to twelve days in the *hielera*;

- ICE [US Immigration and Customs Enforcement] interrogation meeting between immigration judge and asylum seeker is all in English; at times, interpreter doesn't give true interpretation of both Qs and As;

- Often refugee is not given explanation; just told to 'sign here';

- Suspicion of 'business' between judge and lawyer based on conduct between the two;

AUTHOR'S NOTE: One client paid his lawyer US$5,500 for representation, and lawyer failed to be present for the hearing.

- the aftereffects of being in a detention center: disorientation, awakening at 4:00 a.m.–5:00 a.m., headaches, nervousness.

AUTHOR'S NOTE: One earlier detainee reported he required fifteen days of freedom before feeling normal again.

AUTHOR'S NOTE: Worry over a brother and cousin still detained.

QUESTION TO THE READER: With this kind of treatment of the asylum seeker, it's very difficult to say, 'Welcome to America!' Isn't it?

■ ■ ■

Life-threatening

I am a twenty-eight-year-old Nicaraguan, having lived in Costa Rica part of my twenty-eight years. My name is Eri J. Rojas, a farmer with a ninth-grade education, a wife, and two daughters. I was identified as participating in the political opposition by supporting the students in sit-ins and marches. I was investigated various times and threatened with enforced disappearance.

Leaving Nicaragua on January 16th, I passed through Mexico and reached the US on February 27th. The *coyotes* (smugglers) charged me US$2,000 to cross me at Roma, Texas. I was picked up by the *migra* (immigration authorities), and they kept me in the *hielera* (cold storage detention room) for fourteen days, in constant cold and under the intense glare of lights 24/7. During those two weeks, I was fed water, crackers, and bread. I was being starved. I couldn't walk; they rushed me to a McAllen, Texas, hospital and immediately began giving me saline solution. The doctors started a regimen of twenty-five milligrams of Meclizine, [an antihistamine used to treat motion sickness or vertigo], even though they said, 'It probably won't help you.' I'm still dizzy.

After four days in the Port Isabel Detention Center, I'm here in the Brownsville bus station, ready to go live with my sister in Orlando, Florida, on April 2nd. But, I'm still dizzy and can barely walk.

■　■　■

That's a Lie

I am forty-seven-year-old Élmer Vásquez from Tegucigalpa, Honduras, with just a primary school education, and four sons. I had political problems in Honduras. In addition, there was the situation of the *pandillas* (gangs) who kidnapped my older brother, threatened to kill me, and robbed me of my home and properties. It was time for me to leave Honduras, the most corrupt country in Central America.

I left Honduras by bus on June 6, 2019, traveling all the way through Mexico to Reynosa, Mexico, on a trip without problems which was arranged by a *coyote* (smuggler) for US$10,000. I crossed the Rio Grande in a *lancha* (launch). The *migra* (border patrol) took me to their headquarters in McAllen, Texas, where I stayed forty-seven days, forty-five of which I was in the *hielera* (cold storage detention room) where the conditions were terrible. With the intense cold and 24/7 glaring light, and the poor and meager food rations, I lost forty-five pounds. I was unable to take a bath, brush my teeth, or allowed to make a phone call. Some of my mates tried suicide—slashing their wrists, continuously crying, and going crazy.

We were transferred to a warehouse type building in McAllen where we were kept in wire cages divided by sex and age. One day, Vice President Pence came to visit. I was standing near the cage's wire grid where he stopped, and then asked the group leader how long they kept an individual there. 'Oh,' the tour leader said, 'Not more than eight to ten days.' 'That's a lie,' I shouted out. 'I've been here forty-five days, and I still don't know when I'm being released.' My sister later told me she saw my encounter on both CNN and Telemundo.

I was then moved to the Port Isabel Detention Center on September 23rd. Once again, I was put in the *hielera*, this time only for nine days. While there, I developed a high fever and the mumps in the extreme cold. I lost the hearing in my right ear. I was taken to a specialist at Valley Baptist Hospital in Harlingen, but after examining me, he said there was nothing he could do to help me.

So here I am on December 4th in Brownsville, Texas, at the Good Neighbor Settlement House, after all these experiences. I leave for New York City tonight by bus. I will live with my family and older brother who's worked as a chef for twenty-five years. Perhaps I can get a job in his restaurant's kitchen.

■ ■ ■

Five-month-old Baby Facing Heart Operation Detained in "Hielera" (Cold Storage Detention Room) for Five Days

Our family is from Quito, Ecuador, with five members: namely, Luis Soto, thirty-six years old, with thirteen years of education; Lysia Quishpilemo, thirty-five years old, with thirteen years of education; Leandro, fifteen years old; Antony, nine years old; and Miller, five months old.

I am a man of many talents! I am a truck driver, brick mason, electrician, plumber, and house painter. Quito is a city of much violence and lack of security. The *pandillas* (gangs) are running wild. The police are of no help because they are on the *pandillas'* payroll. One *pandilla* wanted me to join them and sell drugs, threatening me if I didn't join. That's when I decided to flee with my family.

On September 4, 2019, we flew to Cancún, Mexico, and then flew on to Monterrey, Mexico. From Monterrey, we bused to Reynosa, arriving on September 14th. We stayed in a private home for four days, and on September 19, 2019, we crossed the bridge to McAllen, Texas, and were taken to the Border Patrol/Immigration headquarters. We were there for five days. The entire time was spent in the *hielera* (cold storage detention room). Having heard of the extreme cold of the *hielera* from previously talking among fellow asylum seekers in Reynosa, we immediately protested because of our son's heart condition for which we were going to New York City for an immediate operation. The guard's reply was, "Sorry, everyone goes through the *hielera* . . . no excuses!" You can imagine the fear and helplessness my wife and I felt.

Being Evangelical Christians, we knew that the Lord Jesus would never have allowed that, and we could only have faith that God would protect our baby, Miller.

Miller came through that inhumane ordeal okay, and we were allowed to send him and his two brothers to New York to live with my sister-in-law in Queens. We were returned to Matamoros, Mexico, where we stayed in a tent city for three-and-a-half months. The volunteers from *Team Brownsville* were wonderful in providing two hot meals daily, clothes, shoes, blankets, rain gear, and educational activities for adults, youth, and children. At 6:40 a.m. today, January 15th, we crossed the bridge to Brownsville, Texas. Now we are here at the Good Neighbor Settlement House and will fly to New York City tonight, in time to be present for Miller's operation at 7:00 a.m. tomorrow!

■　■　■

Carolyn Cole/Los Angeles Times via Getty Images
RIO GRANDE RIVER
A group of Honduran and Cuban migrants cross
the Rio Grande River on the US–Mexico border
June 26, 2019

Chapter 8

DREAMS

"Joseph had a dream, and when he told it to his brothers, they hated him all the more. He said to them, 'Listen to this dream I had: We were binding sheaves of grain out in the field when suddenly my sheaf rose and stood upright, while your sheaves gathered around mine and bowed down to it.'

His brothers said to him, 'Do you intend to reign over us? Will you actually rule us?' And they hated him all the more because of his dream and what he had said. Then he had another dream, and he told it to his brothers. 'Listen,' he said, 'I had another dream, and this time the sun and moon and eleven stars were bowing down to me.' When he told his father as well as his brothers, his father rebuked him and said, 'What is this dream you had? Will your mother and I and your brothers actually come and bow down to the ground before you?' His brothers were jealous of him, but his father kept the matter in mind."

GENESIS 37:5–11
New International Version (NIV) Bible

To Help My People

JAMES PACE:

His name was Brilliant Kelly, from Cameroon. He had left home because he was a student activist under increasing government pressure. Flying to Ecuador, he then came to the US by bus and on foot. (I wondered, why Ecuador? . . . then remembered, it was a refuge for leftist politicians.). He was going to live with his uncle in Columbus, Ohio, the home of Ohio State University. He wanted to major in history, economics, and government. I asked him if he wanted to remain in the US as a professor.

BRILLIANT KELLY:
No, I'm going to return to Cameroon to help the people of my community.

■ ■ ■

To Help My Father

My name is Marta Miriam Ramírez, a twenty-five-year-old from El Salvador. I finished the twelfth grade of high school, and then went to work in a restaurant as a cook. My father, Estanislao, is a sixty-eight-year-old farmer who has been farming all his life.

The main reason I came to America is to help my father economically. He's in poor health, and finds it very difficult to keep farming. So I left El Salvador by auto on September 24, 2019. I paid a *coyote* (smuggler) US$4,000 to get me to the US. The *coyote* had to pay off the federal highway police in Mexico to allow us to pass.

On October 22nd, I crossed the Rio Grande in a launch from nearby Reynosa, Mexico, and after walking two hours, we surrendered to the *migra* (border patrol) who took us to their headquarters in McAllen, Texas. There the authorities put only me in the *hielera* (cold storage detention room) for two hours because I am four months pregnant. From there, I was passed through a new tent city in Donna, Texas, and then to the Brownsville bus station. Then on to the Good Neighbor Settlement House. I'll leave by bus at 10:00 p.m. tonight for Seattle, Washington, to live with a friend who has two daughters. I want to get a job in a restaurant as quickly as possible to start sending money home to my papa.

■　■　■

My Dreams

At sixteen years old and living in Cuba, I learned to fly and continued to fly as a pilot for sport until I was eighteen. Then for the next eighteen years, I was both a skydiver and glider. I worked for a Cuban government company as a gliding and free-fall instructor. Would you believe my monthly pay was $300 Cuban Pesos, the equivalent of US$ 15.00? My pseudonym is Jesse González, forty-seven years old, with my dad and two brothers still living in Cuba.

I left Cuba for two reasons: political and economic. Today there is no liberty in Cuba. The present national leaders, beginning with the president, are merely puppets, ruled by Fidel's brother, Raúl Castro. The political-economic future is very uncertain. A change in the social vision and the economic system will require a radical change in government. There is no realistic hope for that to happen any time soon.

Spending fifty days in the Port Isabel Detention Center was okay; I have no complaints. My economist wife of five years, Iris Bárbara, accompanied me to the US, and was only in the same detention center for eleven days. Upon release, she traveled to Colorado. I'm flying to be with her tomorrow, January 24th. I can hardly wait to hug and kiss my beloved.

I'll get a job as soon as possible in whatever is available (a store, restaurant, gasoline station). My wife will also be looking for work. I'm determined to be a better man every day. My dreams? I want to compete this year in the USIS Nationals Indoor Skydiving Competition in Florida. I also want to see the *America by Air* exhibit with the history of US aviation. It will be so wonderful to fulfill my dreams!

▪ ▪ ▪

To Be an Educator

My name is Oseas Renan (a pseudonym). I am a twenty-seven-year-old Cuban from the city of Santiago de Cuba. My father is a grocer, working in a government-owned grocery store. No doubt about it, I am a mama's boy. She is the precious one in my life. I have attained a university degree in special education, and am prepared to teach deaf mute children. I love the little ones. However, I have not been accepted as a teacher in the government school system because I am classified as a *gusano* (traitor), a term used since the beginning of the Cuban Revolution.

As a *gusano*, I am considered an enemy of the state for my political protest activities. As the Cuban political scene became more harsh and severe, we increased our protest activities. I have been clubbed in the streets, detained, and twice jailed for three days, each time without food and water. Since I had no future in Cuba, and the present was intolerable, I decided to leave my motherland.

I left Cuba for [French] Guiana on April 23rd, traveling by air to Guiana, and then by bus and on foot through Brazil, Peru, and up the Pacific coast . . . eleven countries total to reach the US. I avoided jail in Nicaragua as a "traitor to the Cuban Revolution" by taking a launch from Costa Rica through the Pacific Ocean, and bypassing Nicaragua. By traveling with a group of experienced Cubans, I never had to use or pay for a *coyote* (smuggler). Mexico is a safe haven for us Cubans. Both citizens and the government helped us by guaranteeing safe conduct through Mexico, offering food, hospitality, and money, when needed. The Beta Group [Grupo Beta, "the decade-old border unit established by the Mexican government to protect migrants as they make their way north to the US"],[26] in its special program of helping Latino immigrants, contributed greatly to our support, eliminating any need for *coyotes*.

Would you believe I'm going to Las Vegas, Nevada, to live with my uncle? There I'll get any job that doesn't require English to become self-supporting, and at the same time, use the best programs and techniques available to learn English, as quickly as possible. Then I'll get teacher certification in Special Education from the State of Nevada, having met the requirements for additional hours in education. Whew!

I, Oseas Renan, will begin to live my dream of teaching deaf mute children.

■   ■   ■

---

26 Smith, James F. "Mexico's Grupo Beta Tries to Make Life Safer for Migrants." *latimes.com*, 17 June 2001, https://www.latimes.com/archives/la-xpm-2001-jun-17-mn-11542-story.html.

To Live in Peace

I am a twenty-six-year-old Honduran mother with a six-year-old daughter living with her father in Kansas the past month. My pseudonym is Elizabet Sangría. My education gave me the title of Business Expert in a small town in Honduras. My husband owned a small butcher shop which produced a good living for our family. Our business attracted the attention of a local *pandilla* (gang), and they demanded we pay them monthly for protection. We refused to pay, and knew we had to flee. My husband and daughter left our town for the US on January 14, 2019, and I followed on February 7th.

I was scared during my whole trip. I had heard so many stories of what had happened to unaccompanied females. I joined several other women and hired a taxi to travel through Mexico . . . fleeing it several times when we were stopped. In Villahermosa, Tabasco State, Mexico, we were detained by federal police for two days before being released. We were helped by people along the way with food and shelter. We crossed the bridge at McAllen, Texas, enduring the *hielera* (cold storage detention room) for five days, plus one day in the Port Isabel Detention Center. I was released so quickly because I'm pregnant.

What is my dream of living in the US? . . . for the three of us to live in peace, learning English as soon as possible.

■　■　■

To Be a Live Singer for the Lord

I come from the largest group of Central American asylum seekers to the US. I am a twenty-six-year-old male from Padua, Honduras, a town of eight thousand. My name is Raúl Ramos (a pseudonym). I have two sisters; my father is a farmer. I have worked for him driving his six-wheel truck carrying construction and farm supplies, his harvests, and those of neighboring farms.

As a deacon in the local parish of the Catholic church, I am known as an outstanding preacher of the Word of God, but my first love is playing guitar and singing praises to the Lord. For five years, I played and sang in a six-man group: two guitars, banjo, violin, accordion, and piano. Besides playing at mass, we performed at fiestas, *cumpleaños* (birthdays), *quinceañeras* (celebrations of a girl's fifteenth birthday and passage to womanhood), and *actos civiles* (civic functions). Outside of the church, our gigs paid well, but a corrupt police official took more than half of the gig as protection money. None of the group members liked this arrangement, but there was nothing we could do about it.

Recently, I was threatened with a life-or-death situation. Members of a local drug gang approached me to join them and use my dad's truck to make deliveries for them in the province. I stalled them for a time . . . 'I have to think about it.' Finally, I refused to do it, for I told them to deliver illegal drugs would go against what my father had taught me. Their reply was, '*Tú eres un ignorante inocente*' (You are an ignorant innocent). They didn't have to say anything else; I already knew the consequences of my decision. After telling my father I had to flee, I took the bus from Honduras through all the countries to the

US border. I paid $250 Mexican Pesos [US$12] for a launch to cross the Rio Grande, and walked a short distance to get picked up by the *migra* (border patrol). Then I spent five days in the *hielera* (cold storage detention room), with just a T-shirt, no blanket, sleeping on the floor, with only stale, cold baloney sandwiches to eat, and a lavatory to drink from.

I was treated okay after my transfer to El Valle Detention Facility in Raymondville, Texas, for a forty-five day period. Now I'm on my way to live with my cousin in South Carolina, and get a job, perhaps, through my cousin's siding company. In the meantime, I'll look for a musical group to join and start playing my guitar, and singing once again. I am so thankful to be alive, and will sing praises to the Lord forever and forever.

■   ■   ■

BENEDICTION

Our Lord, we are grateful
for the courage and protections
you continue to visit on
these sojourners.
May we receive these stories
as a holy mandate of your Spirit,
mobilizing us to new actions of justice
within our borders,
aimed at showing them and
their fellow travelers
permanent hospitality and
inclusion in our economic, social, and
spiritual communities.
Amen.

- DAN BONNER
YDS MDiv '76, STM '77
President and Lead Strategist
The Center of Urban Congregational Renewal

THE GOOD NEIGHBOR SETTLEMENT HOUSE'S

Refugee Respite Program

Brownsville, Texas

When the surge of asylum seekers arrived to the South Texas border in 2018, Sister Norma Pimentel, Executive Director of Catholic Charities of the Rio Grande Valley and the Humanitarian Respite Center in McAllen, Texas, reached out to Jack White, then Voluntary Interim Director of the Good Neighbor Settlement House in Brownsville, Texas, to address the humanitarian crisis. In Jack White, she discovered a man whose education and work experience could lead Brownsville through the daily reception of up to 150 asylum seekers, after their release from the Immigration and Naturalization Service (INS). White had graduated with a Master of Social Work from the Brown School at Washington University in St. Louis, one of the world's foremost schools for the training of social science researchers. In the 1960s, he had also worked in St. Louis to address low-income housing and urban development projects. In Brownsville, he was a distinguished professor in graduate studies of social work at Texas Southmost College, followed by the University of Texas Rio Grande Valley in Brownsville and Edinburgh.

Sister Pimentel asked White to investigate specifically INS's discharge methods of the asylum seekers at the Brownsville bus station and to implement a better policy. White found the INS was discharging asylees at 9:00 p.m, and no one was available to assist them to make travel connections to their final destinations elsewhere in the US. Often the asylees had to remain overnight at the bus station because of the limited itineraries. White organized a volunteer service group to address the lack of planning, food, clothing, hygiene, and communication. The Refugee Respite program was born in Brownsville. With time, at the urging of the Chief of Police, the INS changed the discharge to 5:30 a.m. White's group of volunteers reorganized, and decided they could better assist the asylum seekers at the Good Neighbor Settlement House's home base, rather than at the bus station. In February, 2019, the INS informed White the refugees would be dropped off directly at the Good Neighbor Settlement House, hundreds at a time. White's small group of staff and community volunteers, including twelve student-interns from the UTRGV School of Social Work, set up the community room to handle the massive influx of men, women, and children—a 24/7 operation. While historic supporters withdrew funding, national news generated contributions and volunteer support, as well as the participation of the City of Brownsville.

By March 2020, the Good Neighbor Settlement House in Brownsville had served over 28,110 refugees from 31 countries. True to its "Settlement Movement" origins of 1955 and the interfaith group of women who raised money to build and operate Brownsville's first settlement house, the Good Neighbor Settlement House once again has embraced people in exile. *Mother of Exiles* brings to life the humanitarian crisis that one small border town in Texas rose up to meet through strength, intelligence, faith, and love.

■ ■ ■

Asylum Seekers
from thirty-one countries

Served by the Good Neighbor Settlement House in Brownsville, Texas, as of March 2020

1. Argentina
2. Bangladesh
3. Brazil
4. Cameroon
5. China
6. Cuba
7. Democratic Republic of the Congo
8. Ecuador
9. El Salvador
10. Eritrea
11. Ethiopia
12. Gambia
13. Georgia
14. Ghana
15. Guatemala
16. [French] Guiana
17. Guyana
18. Honduras
19. India
20. Mexico
21. Nicaragua
22. Peru
23. Romania
24. Russia
25. South Africa
26. Sri Lanka
27. Turkey
28. Uganda
29. Uzbekistan
30. Vietnam
31. Venezuela

References

Origins of the Settlement House Movement, https://socialwelfare.library
.vcu.edu/settlement-houses/origins-of-the-settlement-house-movement/

Good Neighbor Settlement House, https://www.goodneighborsh.org/

United Methodist Women, https://www.unitedmethodistwomen
.org/what-we-do/national. What we fund see: https://www.united
methodistwomen.org/what-we-fund/international-ministries/united
-states-mission-map

Sister Norma Pimentel, Catholic Charities of the Rio Grande, https://
www.unitedmethodistwomen.org/what-we-do/national

Brownsville Metro, "B metro" https://www.cob.us/908/La-Plaza

US Citizenship and Immigration Services https://www.uscis.gov/

Iglesia Bautista West Brownsville, Rev Carlos Navarro; https://iglesia
bautistawb.com/inicio/

Salesforce Worldwide Corporate Headquarters, Woodson Martin https://
www.salesforce.com/

UTRGV Graduate School of Social Work, https://www.utrgv.edu/social
work/

City of Brownsville, Texas, https://www.cob.us/

Acknowledgments

To my parents, James and Zenobia Pace, who laid the foundation from which I come. Their numerous contributions to Brownsville education, charities, and social justice initiatives shaped my world views and values. To my older sister Betty Pace Dodd, who spearheaded the drive to build a modern public library in Brownsville. To Bob Martin, my high school football coach, and Methodist pastor Elmer Hierholzer, my two role models.

To Dr. I.K. Stevens at Southern Methodist University, who introduced me to process philosopher Alfred North Whitehead. To George Fooshee, who exemplifies Christian discipline. To Richard Wilke and Richard Gelwick, friends at SMU and Yale Divinity School. Bishop Richard Wilke and his wife Julia coauthored a comprehensive two-volume study of the Bible. Richard Gelwick's antiracism initiatives stopped the Methodist Church in Virginia from ever supporting segregated schools. At Yale, to three professors: Browne Barr who taught me homiletics; theologian Richard Niebuhr who championed Søren Kierkegaard's *Either/Or*; Charles Foreman, whose global perspective on Christianity influenced my choice to become a missionary near the Amazon basin, not a pastor in the US.

To Bolivia's late Bishop Sante Uberto Barbieri, who focused on God's gift of freedom for all His creation. To the Reverend Murray Dickson, who extended the presence of Methodism in Bolivia, and who shepherded my wife Evelyn and me through the loss of our son, Richard, before his own tragic death.

To Rosa and Bob Caufield, founders of the Rural Institute of Montero. To Patricia and Harry Peacock, who established community development projects for Quechua-speaking and *mestizo* peasants in remote rural areas. To Dr. Jim Alley and his wife, Jean, who implemented effective health programs to reduce child mortality rates and tuberculosis.

To Jack White, volunteer director of the Good Neighbor Settlement House, who founded the Refugee Respite program in 2018. To Marianela Watson, the program's glue that keeps the volunteers together. To Sergio Cordova, who initiated *Team Brownsville* to greet asylum seekers, and feed 2,500 refugees in Matamoros's tent cities. To Melba and David Lucio, who every Sunday bring music, games, and education to all in the tent cities. To Andrea Rudnik, for her interviews of asylum seekers distributed broadly through Facebook. To Martin and Kelly Woodson, for their initial financial support and volunteerism with the asylum seekers. To Pastor Phillip Hoeflinger of the First United Methodist Church for rallying his congregation to provide clothing, food, and contributions to the Refugee Respite program. To Ray Waddle, editor of Yale Divinity School's *Reflections*, whose proximate immigration issue will feature asylum seeker interviews. To Getty Images and AP Photo, for critical editorial photographs. To Justin Barringer, for his insightful manuscript comments. To the Reverend Dan Bonner, who led me back to the Methodist Church, and who contributed to this book. To my beloved children Jim, Suzanne, Sarah, and Rebecca; and stepchildren Kathleen and Scott; and Melanie, for bringing beauty and treasured grandchildren to this world. And to my wife, Darlene, for her unfailing honesty and love.

■　　■　　■

Author's Biography

James Pace was born in 1930 in Brownsville, Texas. He attended Southern Methodist University and graduated cum laude Phi Beta Kappa with a BA in English in 1952. After one year's graduate studies at Durham University in England, he enrolled in the School of Divinity at Yale University, graduating as class president in 1956 with a Master of Divinity. Ordained as a minister in the United Methodist Church, Pace and family were assigned to the eastern Bolivian lowlands of Montero, Santa Cruz. He was founding pastor of the Montero Methodist church, educator in the Methodist high school, community developer, and executive secretary of the Methodist Church in Cochabamba. After ten years, Pace and his family returned to the US. He joined the Teamsters Local 688 in St. Louis, Missouri, as a community organizer and director of political education. In 1972, he returned to Brownsville to work for Pace Fish Company for fifteen years. Not wanting to retire, Pace taught English grammar and literature for eighteen years. In September, 2018, he volunteered to work for the Refugee Respite program at Brownsville's Good Neighbor Settlement House, for as long as it continues.

He has devoted his life to social justice.

■   ■   ■